W9-BNC-902

WITHDRAWN

WITHDRAWN

BUCKNELL REVIEW

Caribbean Cultural Identities

STATEMENT OF POLICY

BUCKNELL REVIEW is a scholarly interdisciplinary journal. Each issue is devoted to a major theme or movement in the humanities or sciences, or to two or three closely related topics. The editors invite heterodox, orthodox, and speculative ideas and welcome manuscripts from any enterprising scholar in the humanities and sciences.

This journal is a member of the Conference of Editors of Learned Journals

BUCKNELL REVIEW
A Scholarly Journal of Letters, Arts, and Sciences

Editor
PAULINE FLETCHER

Associate Editor
DOROTHY L. BAUMWOLL

Assistant Editor
ANDREW P. CIOTOLA

Contributors should send manuscripts with a self-addressed stamped envelope to the Editor, *Bucknell Review*, Bucknell University, Lewisburg, PA, 17837.

BUCKNELL REVIEW

Caribbean Cultural Identities

Edited by
GLYNE GRIFFITH

Lewisburg
Bucknell University Press
London and Toronto: Associated University Presses

© 2001 by Rosemont Publishing & Printing Corp.

Associated University Presses
440 Forsgate Drive
Cranbury, NJ 08512

Associated University Presses
16 Barter Street
London WC1A 2AH, England

Associated University Presses
P.O. Box 338, Port Credit
Mississauga, Ontario
Canada L5G 4L8

The paper used in this publication meets the
requirements of the American National Standard for
Permanence of Paper for Printed Library Materials Z39.48-1984.

(Volume XLIV, Number 2)

ISBN 0-8387-5475-9
ISSN 0007-2869

PRINTED IN THE UNITED STATES OF AMERICA

Contents

Recent Issues of BUCKNELL REVIEW

Notes on Contributors

MIKE ALLEYNE is assistant professor in the Department of Recording Industry at Middle Tennessee State University. His research focuses on the intersection of ideology and popular culture, and his published work includes essays on technology and dub music, and hegemony and the music of Bob Marley.

RICHARD ALLSOPP is professor emeritus at the University of the West Indies, Cave Hill campus, Barbados. A dialectologist and lexicographer, his many publications include the *Dictionary of Caribbean English Usage* published by Oxford in 1996. He is the director of the Caribbean Lexicography Project and is completing work on a supplement to the *Dictionary* as well as a text entitled *A Book of Afric-Caribbean Proverbs*.

GLYNE GRIFFITH is associate professor of English at Bucknell University, and his area of research interest is the intersection of literature, ideology, and culture. His several publications on Caribbean literature and culture include *Deconstruction Imperialism and the West Indian Novel* (1996), and he is completing a book on the BBC "Caribbean Voices" and the development of West Indian literature.

GEORGE LAMMING is a regionally and internationally recognized novelist, essayist, and public intellectual. His numerous publications include the novels *In the Castle of My Skin* (1953), *Of Age and Innocence* (1958), *Season of Adventure* (1960) and the essay collections *The Pleasures of Exile* (1960) and *Coming Coming Home: Conversations II* (1995). The recipient of several awards and honors including a Guggenheim, a Sommerset Maugham Award, and an honorary doctorate from the University of the West Indies, Dr. Lamming remains actively involved in the cultural and intellectual life of the Americas.

EVELYN O'CALLAGHAN is senior lecturer in the Department of Literatures in English at the Cave Hill campus of the University of the

West Indies, Barbados. A Jamaican Rhodes scholar, professor O'Callaghan's numerous publications on Caribbean women's writing and culture include *Woman Version: Theoretical Approaches to West Indian Fiction by Women* (1993).

GORDON ROHLEHR is professor of West Indian literature at the St. Augustine campus of the University of the West Indies, Trinidad. An expert on the history and culture of the Calypso, professor Rohlehr's numerous publications include *Calypso and Society in Pre-Independence Trinidad* (1990).

PATRICIA SAUNDERS is assistant professor of English at Bowdoin College. Her research interests include Caribbean women's writing and Jamaican dance hall culture. She is completing a book on the theory and politics of anglophone Caribbean women's writing.

EDDY SOUFFRANT is assistant professor of philosophy at Marquette University. His primary research area is ethics, and he has a particular interest in Haiti and issues of colonialism and imperialism. His several publications in this area include *Formal Transgression: John Stuart Mill's Philosophy of International Affairs* (2000).

Introduction

Glyne Griffith

T HE theme of this issue of the *Bucknell Review* is "Caribbean Cultural Identities," and each analysis might be understood to be responding to the questions, What does it mean, culturally and philosophically, to be a Caribbean person, and what are some of the significant historical and ontological premises informing Caribbean identity construction? The first three presentations, those by George Lamming, Richard Allsopp, and Gordon Rohlehr, were originally delivered as public lectures under the auspices of the University of the West Indies Humanities Festival at the Barbados campus of the U.W.I.[1] These lectures have been transcribed for inclusion in this issue on Caribbean cultural identities because they are pertinent, previously unpublished analyses of the topic provided by leading Caribbean intellectuals. In addition, as transcriptions of public lectures on the topic of identity in the Caribbean, these three essays may be said to offer an approximation of Caribbean "voice" on the page, and indeed, one of the means by which Caribbean identity is perhaps most readily discerned is in the "voicing" of language, not just as a consequence of cadence and inflection, but also as a result of idiom and metaphor.

The other essays presented in this issue are representative of insightful, contemporary scholarly work on the nature of Caribbean culture and Caribbean identity. Although each analysis might be said to vary somewhat in terms of narrative focus, style, and disciplinary grounding, the common thread uniting this collection into a coherent whole is the intellectual concern with the complex and oftentimes vexed question of identity in a Caribbean cultural and philosophical context.

George Lamming's lecture "Caribbean Labor, Culture, and Identity" begins by lamenting Caribbean social science's extraordinary reliance on statistical analysis as the primary means of comprehending and defining Caribbean cultural reality. Lamming argues, for example, that there is "little evidence that the [Sir Arthur Lewis] Institute of Social and Economic Research [at the University of the West

Indies] has ever really seriously regarded culture as an area of social research. It still unfortunately tends to be constrained within a statistical prison that has not allowed for that kind of vision of culture." Proceeding from this lament of typical social science methodology in the Caribbean, Lamming maps a simultaneously autobiographical and historical journey of the humanities in the Caribbean and manages to successfully integrate cultural and historical routes as varied as the "invisibility" of Indian labor in Trinidad, the collapse of the 1950s political experiment in Guyana, the "Old World" sensibilities of Christopher Columbus, and the challenges faced by the University of the West Indies at the end of the twentieth century.

Richard Allsopp's lecture "Caribbean Identity and Belonging" begins by exploring the genealogy of the term *Caribbean*. Proceeding from Columbus's navigational miscalculation which, nevertheless, as a consequence of European hegemony, would produce the linguistic and epistemological truth of the "West Indies," Allsopp explores the soul-destroying legacy of plantation slavery for blacks in the Caribbean. Highlighting some of the ways in which slavery produced black self-hatred and left the trace of such denegration in Caribbean English, for example, "black and ugly, black and stupid, black and ignorant, black and lazy, black and wutliss [worthless]," Allsopp disputes the claim that in terms of cultural and historical experience the European enslavement of blacks in the Americas is comparable to the consequent indentureship of Indians in the Caribbean. Allsopp argues that the negative stereotypes of blacks as ignorant and lazy, stereotypes consolidated during plantation slavery, would be pressed into service by indentured labor in the Caribbean to serve, inter alia, the reification of racial and ethnic notions of Caribbean identity constructions.

Gordon Rohlehr's lecture considers the role of the calypso in Caribbean culture and indicates that the calypso mirrors and simultaneously comments on Caribbean identity as socially and historically constructed. Rohlehr suggests that the calypso tends to place particular emphasis on the role of race and ethnicity in the construction of Caribbean identities. A significant part of the grand question this analysis poses is, How does one understand a Caribbean and define a Caribbean identity in a region that is multiethnic, multilingual, multicultural, and ideologically plural? In addition, Rohlehr surmises that these complex differences help to make the region more exploitable and prone to ideological manipulation from external cultural influences since there is no commonly accepted core of values which might serve to counteract such extraregional influences.

Rohlehr argues that the calypso in Trinidad evolved out of a multicultural, multiethnic context and, indeed, continues to evolve as a Caribbean musical idiom. In its earliest forms, he suggests, it employed Orisha chants grounded in Yoruba traditions but taken out of their original cultural context and set to different drum rhythms. This experimentation, he argues, may have provided the basis for the early minor-key melodies of the stick-fighting songs. Rohlehr indicates that the musical structure of the calypso was "the fundamental structure of a wide variety of African musics of the so-called call and response or clergy/laity form." Rohlehr's analysis of Caribbean identity, explored through the medium of the calypso, might be suitably comprehended by considering his own statement: "I am insisting that in looking at the origin and the structure of calypso music, we are in fact looking at the deep structure, in the linguistic sense of that term, of Caribbean society and identity."

Evelyn O'Callaghan's essay considers the problematic of Caribbean identity through the medium of literature and with a gesture toward postmodernism's idea of identity as dynamically unstable, fractured, and decentralized. Focusing on Anglophone Caribbean fiction published since 1987, O'Callaghan observes that the idea of homelessness is not the conundrum for recent authors of Caribbean fiction that it was for the exiled characters in, say, Sam Selvon's *The Lonely Londoners* or Claude McKay's *Home to Harlem.* Paying particular attention to V. S. Naipaul's *The Enigma of Arrival,* Jamaica Kincaid's *Lucy,* and David Dabydeen's *The Intended,* O'Callaghan suggests that:

> Most of the writers mentioned above obviously have a quite different relationship with the "mother country" or "metropole" or "imperial center" than did the West Indian authors who migrated to England or the United States in the 1950s . . . In varying ways, the protagonists of the newer texts, as much as their authors, are at home in the center, or, put another way, they are as homeless there as in any other place.

Thus the idea of the West Indian's "home" as some stable, geographically fixed location becomes increasingly untenable, and if this is so, as O'Callaghan suggests, then one can surmise that the idea of Caribbean identity and Caribbean culture as some set of clearly definable features and practices is itself complicated by discourses that feature destabilization and decentralization as significant themes.

The essay by Eddy Souffrant also begins with a gesture toward ideas popularized by postmodernism. Starting with a general discussion of the postmodernist notion, popularized by thinkers such as Jean-François Lyotard, that the grand narratives of history and identity are defunct, Souffrant engages instead the ideas of Cornel West and Paul Gilroy in order to move toward an ontological analysis of Caribbean identity configurations. Souffrant addresses three categories of identity formation: *national identity, contact identity,* and *composite identity.* He suggests that if one considers the ways in which nationality and the legal ramifications of nationality have been historically deployed in regions such as the Caribbean in order to circumscribe and delimit movement of specific peoples into and out of national borders, one begins to comprehend the manner in which certain identity constructions might be said to be *negatively* formed. Souffrant states:

> Consider an interesting example of the problem of identity. The country of Colombia publishes a list of countries whose citizens, if they wish to visit that country, are required to have the prospective host country's approval for entry. Citizens of Haiti, the Dominican Republic, Cuba and China and several other countries are expected to prove good health, economic solvency, produce a legitimate invitation to that country, etc. But curiously, not found on this list are countries such as France, whose imposing policies impact nefariously on the peoples of Togo, Algeria and the Middle East, for example; the United States whose contemporary foreign policies have been less than altruistic; the former Soviet Union, Germany, Israel, Portugal, Spain, Belgium, etc.

Thus, Souffrant argues, a Haitian identity that is grounded in historical and political narratives such as the Columbian list suggests, would constitute an identity established upon the ground of an externally imposed negativity. The essay goes on to argue instead for the notion of a *transitional* or *diasporic* identity, a concept grounded in the dynamic of sociopolitical exigencies and thus a concept which remains philosophically superior to negative identity impositions as well as essentialist identity constructions based primarily on spurious claims of uniqueness.

Shifting to a discussion of aspects of popular culture in the Caribbean, Mike Alleyne's essay focuses on the intersection of music and album cover imagery in the English-speaking Caribbean. The essay begins by lamenting the relatively clichéd and stereotyped images used on album covers to advertise much Caribbean music and considers that the mass market shift from the album jacket to the CD "jewel box" has potentially exacerbated an already difficult situation regarding potentially innovative cover imagery:

> The inevitable reduction of cover size on the CD insert versus the vinyl album sleeve is a crucial issue. It provides both a symbolic indication of

a confining reduction of artistic scope and options within the music industry's mainstream, and an inversely disproportionate representation of the ever-growing dominance of visual media as gateways to aural art.

Highlighting abstraction as one aspect of a potentially innovative use of the CD insert's limited canvas, Alleyne's essay concludes that several dub music inserts as well as some of the calypso/soca offerings from Eddy Grant's Ice Records appear to facilitate the most fruitful readings of CD cover imagery in Anglophone Caribbean popular music.

Returning to literary analysis, Patricia Saunders analyzes the "project of becoming" in Marlene Nourbese-Philip's *Discourse on the Logic of Language* and Erna Brodber's *Louisiana*. In this essay, Saunders argues that the wave of Caribbean women's writing which has, in a manner of speaking, superceded that first wave of male-dominated writing of the preindependence period of Caribbean history is characterized by its critical and creative deformation of traditional notions of nation and nationality:

> Several women writers have engaged the ideological and political silences in nationalist movements with respect to questions of ethnicity, gender, and class. Their representations of these critical questions highlight the contradictory nature of claims made in the name of the nation and its subjects.

Saunders argues that whereas Nourbese-Philip's work engages the links between the violence of foreign language as imposition and the violence of sexual exploitation, Brodber's work explores the "silences" which are discernible in postcolonial, nationalist narratives. Nevertheless, both writers, Saunders suggests, share a similar concern with eschewing binarist notions of Caribbean identity formation in order to move toward a more creative and liberating concept of Caribbean womanhood and personhood.

Finally, Glyne Griffith's essay examines two Caribbean narratives, Hilary Beckles's historical text, *Natural Rebels: A Social History of Enslaved Black Women in Barbados* and Earl Lovelace's novel, *The Wine of Astonishment*. Griffith argues that both narratives struggle with discursive structures which by their very nature challenge each narrative's desire to foreground the agency and personhood of their respective Caribbean protagonists. The relative success of each tale told is thus discovered in the respective narrative's own struggle with the discourse out of which it evolves. The essay concludes with the suggestion that perhaps those narrative approaches which are characterized by discursive and disciplinary hybridity might best represent the complex dynamic of Caribbean identity formations.

GLYNE GRIFFITH

Notes

1. These lectures were delivered to mark the inaugural Humanities Festival held at the Cave Hill campus of the University of the West Indies, Barbados, in March 1994. The lectures are included in this issue on Caribbean cultural identities because the analyses provided are not "dated" by the circumstance of their original presentation. The lectures by George Lamming and Richard Allsopp provide critical insight into the long history of racial and cultural tension between Indo-Trinidadians and Afro-Trinidadians and Indo-Guyanese and Afro-Guyanese, respectively. Indeed, Allsopp's analysis responds to Lamming's critique at several points, and both analyses are very relevant to the racial and cultural issues that haunt Trinidad and Guyana even now. The lecture by Gordon Rohlehr offers relevant critical insight into the intersection of calypso and Caribbean cultural identity while also considering the uneasy relationship between calypso and soca on one hand, and calypso and chutney on the other.

BUCKNELL REVIEW

Caribbean Cultural Identities

Caribbean Labor, Culture, and Identity

George Lamming

Introduction

B EFORE addressing concerns relating to Caribbean identity, the question of a festival of the humanities also concerns me. I was asking my host whether this was the first humanities festival at the University of the West Indies, and I was both surprised to hear that it was the first such festival at the institution and puzzled that some institution called a university, existing for almost four or five decades, should have its first humanities festival in 1994. And then I am curious as to the extraordinary, euphoric response to the fascinating series of lectures on cricket, in the name of and on behalf of Sir Garfield Sobers. [During 1994, there was a series of radio broadcasts on West Indies cricket presented in honor of legendary Barbadian cricketer, Sir Garfield Sobers.] I have listened very carefully to the series of broadcasts on the radio, and what I'm struck by is the thematic repetition of these lectures. They do not vary in any emphasis; there is no variation in theme, and you get the feeling that there is a theme to be presented to the society which could only be presented in the capsule of cricket if it were to be digestible to that society. An interesting paradox here is that what the lectures are critiquing is the very code within which they are constrained. The theme is the role of race as a material form of expression in the determining of social relations and individual attitudes. But that obviously could not be presented with approvable posture, if put in that way. Cricket is the capsule that makes it digestible.

In addition, the fascinating blend of alcohol and the cricket bat and ball, with cricket symbolized by the face of Sir Garfield Sobers appearing as an advertisement strategy on bottles of that most popu-

---

This essay was originally presented as the keynote address at the University of the West Indies first Humanities Festival on 6 March 1994 at the Cave Hill campus, Barbados. A few passages in the original text have been deleted or slightly altered by the editor of this volume.

lar of Barbadian spirits, rum, is the sort of thing that would be very worthy of research, if the Institute of Social and Economic Research at the University of the West Indies could make a departure from its normal statistical preoccupations. There is little evidence that the Institue of Social and Economic Research has ever seriously regarded culture as an area of social research. It still, unfortuately, tends to be constrained within a statistical prison that has not allowed for that kind of vision of culture. What I want to do now, therefore, is not so much to lecture, but to take you on a kind of journey which I comprehend as the ongoing theme of what I call the humanities.

If we have at one and the same time embarked on such a journey and indulged in regret about it, we understand that it is a journey which is both autobiographical and historical. In addition, I also want to say something else in relation to the cricket lecture series I mentioned above. It is an observation which is rather different from what I am going to focus on, but it is pertinent to this main focus, and it derives from an interesting comment cited by the historian Edward Hallet Carr in his collection of lectures entitled *What Is History?* In this text, Carr indicates that he was reminded by A. E. Houseman, himself a very extraordinary sort of poet and classicist, that for the historian, accuracy is a duty, but it is not a virtue. It is very important to get these priorities right, that is, to determine whether accuracy takes precedence over virtue in the practice of that profession, or whether virtue ought to resist any tendency to be swamped by accuracy.

On an occasion such as this (and I wish to say here that I was born in Barbados, which is not usually believed), I always imagine that I am talking to a composite Caribbean audience. Whether I see you or not, what is in front of me as I speak is Trinidad and Guyana and Jamaica, Cuba, the Dominican Republic, and so on. That is the audience I consider myself to be most obviously addressing. What I want to do or try to do in going through this narrative journey is to pinpoint areas of confrontation within the concept of humanities in order to lead to a possible ideology which a university might have about the concept of the humanities. I assume that since this is the first occasion of a humanities festival at this institution, there may be no clarity about the University of the West Indies relation to that area of commitment.

Indian Presence in the Caribbean

My childhood in Barbados did not have on its agenda any question which related to a concept of the Caribbean beyond the most elementary requirements of geography. Jamaica was remote and derived its reality almost entirely from the achievements of a cricketer named George Headley, whom none of us as young people in Barbados would have seen. Guyana, better known then as a place called Demerara, was a place where people in distress often went to consult with obeah men on questions of marriage and the inheritance of property. If you were in any doubt about "catching" your man or woman, you went to Demerara to get advice on this. Trinidad was a more frequent experience due largely to annual visits of people who were then called tourists. The Trinidadians are no longer tourists, but this territory was at that time a place to be wary of, since the name "Trinidad" was associated with trickery, sexual license, and a general resistance to all forms of order. That is why during those earlier times the policemen in Trinidad were often recruited from Barbados. Richard Allsopp [U.W.I. professor emeritus and Caribbean dialectologist] may correct me on this, but there also may have been another reason for that mutual apprehensiveness between Barbados and Trinidad because I discovered by a peculiar kind of transmission of oral history that the Trinidadian term "badjohn" [a colloquialism for that type of man who is unruly and with whom one does not trifle] derives from *bajan* [an Anglophone Caribbean colloquialism for Barbadians]; these bajans were in fact reputed to be the most difficult animals that the law had to deal with in Laventille, Trinidad.

In the case of my boyhood/schoolhood recollections, what I am describing is an acute form of insularity which was cultivated in Barbados as a virtue: it was a virtue to be insular. We believed all these things to be true because we were taught that we occupied a place of special favor in the judgment of the ruling Empire. It was the careful work of systematic cultural indoctrination. But if this insularity assumed an extreme form in Barbados, the experience of travel would later warn me that it was, in varying degrees, a fairly general condition throughout the Caribbean region.

If the metropole once encouraged it as a strategy for divide and rule, we Caribbean peoples would later convert it into a convenient device for electoral advantage, until the supreme triumph of backwardness, self-imposed, was realized in the creation of a series of independent ministates, more dependent, more vulnerable, more mendicant than their authors could have imagined. Our particular multiparty system, with its seasonal "cockfights" for political office, offered us an experiment in democratic participation, but became the most effective instrument of national and regional divisiveness.

My childhood in Barbados did not evoke in me any awareness of

an Indian presence in the Caribbean or the concept of the Caribbean as a concrete human reality; yet today, I hold no stronger conviction than that the Caribbean is our own experiment in a unique
equation of human civilization. My experiences in Trinidad (to
which I owe deep-felt gratitude), not in Barbados, first awoke in me
an awareness of this Caribbean world. It started in 1946 with my introduction to Trinidadian families, who were largely of African visibility. It was not always easy for the untutored eye to detect the other
ingredients, and I could not always tell who were or were not Indian.
They were faces totally black, with a slant of eyes and rigidity of
cheekbone which belonged, it seemed, to another race. But it was
not the evidence of miscegenation that fascinated so much as the
discovery that many of the households I visited during that time
were, in fact, a family of islands. The mother in the house would be
Grenadian, the father Vincentian, the grandfather Barbadian; there
would be an aunt seeking refuge from Antigua, and so on. Sometimes the only Trinidadians by birth were the children. Indeed, perhaps the only real Trinidadians with a length of continuity are Indians. Being the only ones who could trace two or three generations
born in the country, and since this lineage, if we consider this aspect
only, could trace its branches in a variety of territories, it dawned
on me that this region, this Caribbean, was already a fact of continuity.

After what was for me the feudal authority of white Barbados, and
it is difficult to communicate to those who did not live there how
profoundly feudal that authority was, I had some difficulty recognizing which faces in Trinidad were white. There were certainly such
faces, but it seemed as though they moved always through shadows
of some other variety. But throughout those four or five years that I
lived in Trinidad, I existed in an involuntary, almost unconscious,
segregation from the world of Indians in Trinidad. I had not met
any Indians, certainly not through casual encounter or as a result of
common interests, but these individual relationships had a certain
autonomy which did not make for access to that other world of India
in Trinidad. And if I did not enter that world of Indians in Trinidad,
it was also true to say that I never had any experience of rejection by
it. Indeed, that world started to register its absence on me as I became more cognizant of the workplace in certain areas of Trinidadian public life. I rarely, if ever, met an Indian civil servant in the
1940s. I have no recollection of seeing an Indian policeman. But the
reality of that world of India in Trinidad came home to me in the
very early hours before dawn. I used to enjoy what West Indians call
"liming" (an Anglophone colloquialism meaning to "hang out," to

socialize) in a place called St. James. Since I lived in Belmont, I would be returning from St. James somewhere between two and three in the morning. The reality came to me in those early hours when the pavement outside what was then the George Street Market would be crowded with what could barely be perceived as human shapes, and boxes, and crocus bags with every variety of fruit and vegetable the earth could produce—and the shapes, these people in the shadows of early morning, were all Indian traders. I recall that I would, in my innocence, wonder how far they had traveled, when they had started on that journey with such a cargo, and whether the country in which I now lived realized that it was these invisible hands which fed it?

Indian Labor: A Creative Caribbean Reality

If labor is the foundation of all culture, then the Indian presence in Trinidad was the ground floor on which that house was built. Fundamental to all of my thinking, this concept of labor and the relations experienced in the process of labor is the foundation of all culture, and this is crucial to what I mean by the Indian presence as a creative Caribbean reality. For it is through work that men and women make nature a part of their own history. The way we see, the way we hear, our nurtured sense of touch and smell, the whole complex of feelings which we call sensibility, is influenced by the particular features of the landscape which has been humanized by our work; there can be no history of Trinidad or Guyana that is not also a history of the humanization of those landscapes by Indian and other human forces of labor.

I have from time to time taken a view that the most serious obstacle for the realization of the late Eric Williams's triumph as prime minister of Trinidad, and perhaps the greatest explanation for what will have to be seen as his failure to transform the People's National Movement in Trinidad into a national movement, had something to do with the fact that although he recognized the importance of labor, he was not a labor-oriented man. There is no way, in the context of Trinidad, that you could work toward a national movement without coming to a clear understanding of the Indian presence as labor. This had nothing to do with Williams being anti-Indian; he was not pro-black labor either. He simply did not have a labor orientation. This situation was, upon reflection by historians and intellectuals, indeed very sad, because he was at the time and probably still is by today's standards, if you look at who came after, perhaps the most regional of all our leaders in the Caribbean, and the one with the most profound intellectual conviction of the absolute necessity for regionalism.

It was this critical role of labor in the transformation of society which came alive for me again during my first visit to Guyana in the 1950s. These were very, very dark days which revived for me that earlier scene of the "invisible" hands in the George Street Market in Trinidad. It was the experience really of that visit to Guyana that made possible the novel *Of Age and Innocence* in which I was exploring a reflection, and then not very much later, looking at what were the inherent possibilities that existed there in what was then that movement in Guyana of the PPP [People's Progressive Party]. But something quite extraordinary happened in Guyana in the early fifties. What was new and I think without precedent was the forging of two separate armies of labor, African and Indian, into a single political force, and the creation of a consciousness born of that collaboration which led these armies of labor to understand that they were the foundation on which the social order rested. It was, no doubt, this newly forged consciousness that combined with their numerical superiority and the morality of their purpose to equip them to challenge and ultimately dismantle the colonial, authoritarian structure of rule in what was then British Guyana. In the early fifties the People's Progressive Party in Guyana created an environment—expectations and a sense of possiblities—which affected in one way or another every section of the society. It set the agenda of intellectual discourse that influenced the mood and themes of creative expression. This was the soil from which the early and the strongest poems of Guyana's Martin Carter would blossom.

The Creative Potential of Labor

There is for churches and universities an even more precise claim to be made on behalf of organized labor and the informing influence it had on those who have to establish the creative potential of this region in the field of cultural work. It is not often recognized that the major thrust of Caribbean literature in English rose from the soil of labor resistance in the 1930s. The expansion of social justice initiated by the labor struggle had a direct effect on liberating the imagination and restoring the confidence of men and women in the essential humanity of their simple lives. In the cultural history of the region, there is a direct connection between labor and literature, but this dream of Martin Carter suffered a traumatic collapse from which, in my view, the peoples of Guyana have never quite recovered. I am aware of the external forces which were hostile to this dream, the manipulative power of those forces able to intervene and erode what was in the making. However, I do not think we can settle for this as the sole explanation for the collapse of that radical movement against colonialism. A fundamental part of the weakness of that historical moment resulted from the party leadership assuming a human solidarity which had not yet been consolidated. This attribute of human solidarity is not a given; this attribute of human solidarity does not arise by chance or miracle. It has to be learned; it has to be nurtured; it has to be cultivated. This requires a kind of educational work, a kind of indoctrination, the reciprocal sharing of cultural histories which has never been at the center of our political agendas in the Caribbean.

Perhaps there was not time enough. Perhaps it was a misfortune that they came to power, such as it was in 1953. Perhaps the period of opposition, without consuming their energies in the emergencies of administration, might have allowed for that fundamental groundwork in political education and cultural dialogue. This recent consciousness of possiblities among the ranks of labor would have given a new dimension in the most substantial content. Tolerance was the adjustment they made in struggle, but tolerance is a fragile bond, and when the leadership broke, the armies turned with tribal and atavistic fury on each other. We ourselves had fertilized the ground for the enemy to plant further mischief. I think it is a profound illusion and a tragic error to transfer this act of self-mutilation to a foreign conscience we call imperialists. There are certain defeats for which we must be prepared to take full responsibility.

Race: A Force Used to Segregate Labor

The factor we call race has always been a component in our political history. It has been the device which the old plantocracy used to segregate the forces of labor which derived from a different cultural formation. The plantocracy successfully employed such strategies to maintain control over those divisions, and this historical circumstance has been the cultural appeal which certain nationalists, who had no other claims to speak, have made. The consequence of these antagonisms led inevitably to mutual charges of racism. Trinidad, for example, has become increasingly a battleground for this conflict of accusations, but to me it is interesting how Trinidad allows for a certain flexibility in the way these charges are formulated. I take two examples from two distinguished Trinidadians of Indian ancestry. In an interview in the twenty-fifth-independence edition of the *Express* newspaper, Mr. Panday, now Prime Minister of Trinidad and Tobago, states:

> I still maintain that the late Dr. Eric Williams created one of the "most racist" organizations. As I explained earlier, the politics of the society has been organized around the expediency of this political fact. The fact of the matter is that the two numerically dominant groups—the Africans and Indians—have both been disadvantaged as a result of the politics which the Williams design bred.[1]

And in the same newspaper, Kenneth Ramchand, a literary critic and professor of West Indian Literature at the University of the West Indies, indicates that:

> For all of its failings, many of them serious, the party of Dr. Eric Williams must be given credit of a sort. It has never gone so far as to undermine in a decisive way, either the possibility of the idea of racial harmony or the non-partisan status of the army or the police. We take these things for granted at our peril.[2]

I take the word *racism* to have a specific and historical meaning. It defines those individuals and groups who have a profound conviction, accumulated over a long period of time, that they possess an inherent superiority over others, and furthermore they have the power to impose that conviction. It is therefore very different from racial consciousness, and it is not my experience that this kind of conviction informs and determines the relations between Afro- and Indo-Trinidadians. The factor of race as a component in our politics has always given national struggle—even the struggle for equality—a racial component. But the acute sectional rivalry for the distribution of spoils and power in Trinidad does not constitute, in my view, a racist confrontation.

Seeds of Caribbean Identity Formation

A concept of a people or a place does not arise out of the blue. How you come to think of where you are and how you come to think of your relation to where you are is dependent on what is the character and the nature of power where you are situated. You yourself do not, at a certain stage, decide who you are and what your relationship to where you are should be, and it is an illusion to think that you do. These relations are experienced within a specific context of power, and this experience always poses fundamental questions: to what extent have we been able to organize in the interest of our own welfare? to what extent can we control those who have acquired the power to organize our lives?

West Indian economists will frequently identify the problems of scarcity which justify their own professional experience. If you could find a society where there was no problem of scarcity, there could be no such thing as an economist. There would be no raison d'être for the existence of any such expertise. It is the existence of the problem of scarcity that justifies that function, and economists are quick to identify the problems of scarcity. They are much more re-luctant to explore and reveal the nature and the exercise of the power which determines that scarcity. And so, if you are trying to think of concepts of the Caribbean, these concepts you find will un-dergo a certain change. They will differ according to either the cen-ters of power that are shaping them or to the centers of resistance against that power.

If you read the history naively and you hear about a sailor named Columbus whom you receive as hero and discoverer of worlds, your reading participates in a concept that has been shaped by some au-thority. It is very interesting to me, and I hope it will be for you, to draw attention here to two remarkable books carrying exactly the same title—*From Columbus to Castro*—both published in 1970 and written by two distinguished Caribbean scholars: Juan Bosch of Santo Domingo and Eric Williams of Trinidad. Both books were published in the same year, yet neither author was aware that the other was doing the same thing.

The Williams version is a predominantly Anglophone experience. Bosch, however, presents a drama that takes place in what appears to be a Spanish sea. The index of names and places is a remarkable contrast in emphasis. As a result, Bosch offers more of a glimpse of the aboriginal peoples in their response to Spanish invaders than we find in Williams's work, whose book of some five-hundred-odd pages makes only four brief references to the Caribs, a people who had continued to offer the fiercest resistance to the Spanish invaders for more than two hundred years after the arrival of the admiral. Just four references to the Caribs in Williams's *From Columbus to Castro*— yet we have evidence that these people had been around the Ameri-cas from about 300 B.C.; and up until around A.D. 1000, the Caribs were still arriving in the Caribbean.

This cross-fertilization was the seed of our journey, and thus, people who are talking about roots, are not really talking about our formation. This cross-fertilization is the seed of all the journeys, not exclusively the encounter of Europe and Africa or Europe and Asia. And it is this encounter of Europe, Africa, and Asia in the Americas, with its resulting violence, which precipitated Maroon escape from bondage; and, in our time, it is the contemporary challenge of creolization that continues to haunt the energies of many Caribbean writers of African and Indian descent. Within thirty or forty years of the admiral's arrival, we have the almost total destruction of an indigenous population. In other words, what we know of the modern Caribbean, that is, the Caribbean over the last five hundred years, is an area of the world that begins with an almost unprecedented act of genocide. So now what you are talking about or looking at when you contemplate history and the movement of history and the concepts which are used to define historical events depends on the center of power that is your defining marker or the center of resistance that is your redefining marker.

The early arrivants may look heroic if you are looking at one part of what they did. Their achievement in navigation is remarkable; that cannot be devalued or undermined, but at the receiving end, there is a somewhat different story. There is a great deal of repetitive, elaborate complaint and lament about the cruelty of these men in the West Indies. But what I think we sometimes either fail to recognize, or recognize but perhaps do not want to put on the agenda, is their own formation. What sort of world did these men come out of?

If you take, for example, the Dutch historian, Johan Huizinga, you are provided with insight into the cruel harshness of the world from which these men of Europe would come. Here is a passage from Huizinga's *The Waning of the Middle Ages*:

> Tortures and executions are enjoyed by the spectators like an entertainment at a fair . . . The people of Bruges, in 1488, during the captivity of Maximilian, king of the Romans, cannot get their fill of seeing the tortures inflicted, on a high platform in the middle of the market-place, on the magistrates suspected of treason. The unfortunates are refused the deathblow which they implore, that the people may feast again upon their torments.[3]

This is the world, the environment, that shaped the sensibilities of the men who would arrive on the scene in the Americas. And so, what this devastation leaves us with is a territory settled and regimented by those who achieve, lose, and later recover possessions.

What it leaves us with are territories that did not exist in and for themselves; what it leaves us with is the concept of the Caribbean as an imperial frontier.

The Caribbean: An Imperial Frontier

I think that the teachers in our schools, if they are aware of all this, may not always think it prudent to bring home to their students that this history, our history, has been one of almost unprecedented violence. This violence has marked this terrain as imperial frontier: territories of infinite beauty whose material life would be controlled in the interest of a center, we would learn, called the metropole. It is a concept that would be contested by insurrection, by rebellion, by riot, and by intellectual argument from native centers of resistance. The alternative center of resistance has been planted and has gradually expanded. In a way, I suspect there are elements within the university structure of all our territories which have been the agents of this expansion, creating and fertilizing this concept of the Caribbean as one's own historical experience, whose fundamental cultural links are within the region, waiting to be identified and explored. But this legacy of the imperial frontier remains formidable. Yesterday it was Empire; today it is market idolatry. Professor Gordon Rohlehr, in an introduction to a remarkable anthology, *Voice Print*, states in a subdued tone of bitterness that:

> It is only since the 1970s that the term "oral tradition" began to be consistently used in connection with certain developments in West Indian poetry. Before then the debate concerned the viability of "dialect" as a medium for poetry, and was an extension of the troubled issue of the nexus between education, speech, class, status, and power. Creole dialects were thought of as belonging to the semi-literate and poor. To argue, as some linguists did and still do, that Creole is simply another language, neither better nor worse than any other, was to ignore the social and political nature of language. To speak about the vitality and expressiveness of Creole was to sentimentalise warm folksiness without wanting to share in the anguish of its decrepitude, and to display the contempt of a complacent intelligentsia, who secretly wanted to reinforce their superior social status by keeping the mass of the people uneducated.[4]

A very serious problem is articulated here in that there was a strong current within the population which was hostile to the notion of elevating something called dialect and Creole speech.

I will move now into what I consider to be the metaphor at work
in this Caribbean imagination. There seems to me to exist a geography of imagination which imposes on the Caribbean artist a unique
location in time and space. The island is a world whose immediate
neighborhood is the sea. The landscape of the mainland, vast and
cluttered by a great variety of topography, achieves its individuality
by the erection of boundaries and the appropriation of frontiers.
The island knows no boundary except the ocean, which is its gateway to eternity. If the frontier astonishes by its wealth of wonders
and the infinite promise of marvels to be revealed, the island is a
reservoir of secrets. The secret is simultaneously its shield and the
pearl which it is often forced to barter. It is too visible for comfort
and its size makes it vulnerable to the most casual of pirates in pur-
suit of fortune.

There is a peculiar sensibility that is nurtured by this paradoxical
need to participate in novel encounters while it protects that area of
privacy which gives it its special character. The island is a private
place which attracts multiple forms of intrusion. So there is a Caribbean sensibility whose undiscovered history resides in its fiction,
whose history achieves authenticity through the intricacies of metaphor. What the imagination implies achieves a greater force of persuasion for truth than the statistical evidence which measures this
evasive and mesmerizing reality which history records. There is,
therefore, this most paradoxical relation to place where each island
signals the origin of a disaster and is also a seed which fertilizes an
extraordinary faith in the possibility of recovering worlds of the
spirit which yet remain obscured and entombed. A stranger sees
from the cruiseline, now the more fashionable mode of loitering in
the region, these isolated pebbles designed for the casual pleasure
of men and women who seek a temporary distraction from the te-
dium of wealth, but in the imagination of poet Aimé Césaire, for
example, each island is an eye whose gaze the ocean has extended
to embrace all continents as though geography had gone to war:

> Mine too the archipelago bent like the anxious desire for self-negation
> as if with material concern for the most frail slenderness separating the
> two Americas, and the womb which spills towards Europe and the good
> liquor of the Gulf Stream, and one of the two incandescent slopes
> through which the equator walks its tight rope to Africa. And my un-
> fenced island, its bold flesh upright at the stern of the Polynesia, and
> right before it, Guadeloupe split in two by its dorsal ridge, and as misera-
> ble as we ourselves; Haiti where Negritude stood up for the first time and
> swore by its humanity; and the droll little tail of Florida where a Negro

is being lynched, and Africa caterpillaring gigantically up to the Spanish foot of Europe: its nakedness where the scythe of Death swings wide. And I say to myself Bordeau and Nantes and Liverpool and New York and San Francisco. Not a corner of this world but carries my fingerprint.[5]

This theme of the inward journey is taken up by one of the most extraordinary intellectuals of this region, Fernando Ortiz, and there is a work of his which I believe should be at the center of reading for any scholar of the Caribbean, *Cuban Counterpoint*.[6] In this work, Ortiz looks at the evolution of a Caribbean society through the lens of two crops, sugar and tobacco. Through this lens, Ortiz arrives at a notion with which I want to conclude. It is an idea that separates us from the traditional concept of humanities, and brings us, not to the notion of acculturation, but to the idea of transculturation—the notion that if you consider what was already the mixed element in the people who came, and if you consider what was already the mixed elements in the very early stages of arrival, what you then observe is not only what impact x had on y, but also importantly what influence y had on x. This notion, which I think should be at the heart of the concept of the humanities—and which of course it would have been difficult for Europe to acquire—presents us with a particular and special kind of opportunity.

Caribbean Transculturation

This conjuncture of worlds, Amerindian, European, African, and Asian, concentrated within this enclosure, reveals this persistent feature which is a continuing challenge to the native imagination, and I refer to the depth and durability of European hegemony. Thus Columbus was not only a courageous sailor, but a leader and the emissary of a new epoch. He was the carrier of a virus to which the people of the Caribbean would have no adequate immune response. The fundamental truth behind such conclusions is that this materialism, linked to human progress, allowed the Western world to accept that even the enslavement of a people was morally justifiable if it contributed to the march toward economic development, so that the universalizing power of capital reduced labor to a state of fugitive suspense.

Our concept of the humanities, shaped by the European Renaissance from the fifteenth century onwards, and the concept from which this institution, the University of the West Indies, would have been founded, was intended to provide some concrete insight into the nature of the human mode of being. What did it mean to be human? It is a concept which was intended to provide us some perspective from which we might be able to understand human life as a total meaning, expressed in the various manifestations which human existence might take, so that through the intellectual disciplines of art, music, history, religion, and philosophy we would acquire the necessary data which would illuminate all those issues relating to the fundamental question of being human. But for the greater part of the Western triumph that I have been discussing above, this data was circumscribed by those perceptions which had emerged almost exclusively from the Hebraic, Greek, and Christian forms of culture. Indeed, this data would acquire the authority to establish the normative meanings and definitions of all human worlds. It means, therefore, that an enormous body of scholarship and the intellectual staples through which almost everybody taught in these institutions would have been shaped fell within the context of this ideological construct. This concept of the humanities, therefore, has a history that is inseparable from the history of Western imperialism from the fifteenth century to the present. The world was divided between the West and those imperial "others."

There is a story of the Nigerian poet, dramatist, and essayist, Nobel laureate, Wole Soyinka, which illustrates what I'm saying. Soyinka was invited to give a series of lectures at Cambridge University, and when he arrived, he discovered that the faculty members of the Department of English were surprised that he had chosen to lecture on African literature, though he was at the time a professor of literature in Nigeria. Cambridge did not yet consider or had not yet arrived at considering that there was such a category as African literature. When he decided not to go on with the lectures, they asked him to stay, but arrangements were made for the lectures to be given under the auspices of the Department of Anthropology.

Alternatively, our own experience of the Fernando Ortiz concept of transculturation in the Caribbean would help to put some distance between ourselves and that ideological construct which is so fundamental to experiences such as Soyinka's at Cambridge. In a similar regard, I once received a letter from a graduate student with whom I had been working in Miami. The student, who was in the Department of Anthropology at a university there, told me of a Japanese lady who was having some trouble because she had asked to do an anthropological study on an English community but was informed that there was no way that any such study could be done because no such community existed. These questions of the boundaries and the borders of the humanities are, I think, very urgent, since the university, and here I am speaking of the University of the West Indies, as an intellectual community, will find that it has to operate in the context of an increasingly aggresive market ideology.

In this connection, I would like to draw your attention to some of the conflicts and contradictions raised by the American economist Kenneth Galbraith in an interesting work, *The New Industrial State*. These conflicts and contradictions have to do with what we imagine to be free choice and the organized management of consumer demand:

> But there remain more general sources of conflict between the educational and scientific estate . . . One is the management of individual behavior. In the absence of a clear view of the nature of this conflict, much of the dispute centers not on its ultimate causes but on the techniques of management. Management requires extensive access to means of communication—newspapers, billboards, radio and especially television. To insure attention these media must be raucous and dissonant. It is also of the utmost importance that this effort convey an impression, however meretricious, of the importance of the goods being sold. The market for soap can only be managed if the attention of consumers is captured for what, otherwise, is a rather incidental artifact. Accordingly, the smell of soap, the texture of its suds, the whiteness of textiles treated thereby and the resulting esteem and prestige in the neighborhood are held to be of the highest moment. Housewives are imagined to discuss such matters with an intensity otherwise reserved for unwanted pregnancy and nuclear war. Similarly with cigarettes, laxatives, pain-killers, beer, automobiles, dentrifices, packaged foods and all other significant consumer products . . . The economy for its success requires organized public bamboozlement.[7]

And finally, Galbraith speculates on a matter that I think would be very close to our own experience when he says that where the society approves and applauds money-making as the highest social purpose, public servants will often think it appropriate that they sell themselves or their decisions for what they are worth to the buyers.

Now here is a central paradox for the University of the West Indies as an intellectual community which is called upon to train people in the skills which support this system. Here is a critical challenge for this university as an intellectual community in its intercourse with the advertising complex which has, and will continue to have, a power to determine the scale, the content, and the direction of all cultural activity.

Notes

1. *The Sunday Express Independence Magazine*, 30 August 1987, 46–47.
2. Ibid., 17–18.

3. Johan Huizinga, *The Waning of the Middle Ages: A Study of the Forms of Life, Thougt and Art in France and the Netherlands in the Dawn of the Renaissance* (New York: Double-day Anchor Books, 1954), 24.

4. In Stewart Brown, Mervyn Morris, and Gordon Rohlehr, eds., *Voice Print: An Anthology of Oral and Related Poetry from the Caribbean* (Essex: Longman Caribbean Writers, 1989), 1.

5. Aimé Césaire, "Notebook of a Return to the Native Land," in *Aimé Césaire: The Collected Poetry*, trans. Clayton Eshleman and Annette Smith (Berkeley: University of California Press, 1983), 47.

6. Fernando Ortiz, *Cuban Counterpoint: Tobacco and Sugar*, trans. Harriet de Onis (New York: Knopf, 1949).

7. John Kenneth Galbraith, *The New Industrial State* (Boston: Houghton Mifflin, 1967), 293.

Caribbean Identity and Belonging

Richard Allsopp
University of the West Indies, Cave Hill, Barbados

*C*ARIBBEAN, *identity, belonging* are three words that present multifarious difficulties: *Caribbean,* for instance, I pronounce not to pattern with "European" but with American, Canadian, Grenadian, Bahamian, etc., inflection, with the stress on the second syllable. The term, of course, is a mistake, but one that Columbus covered sensibly by calling the region the "West Indies." If he had not taken back some brown-skinned individuals as proof that he did find the "Indians" he had gone to look for, he would probably have lost his head. Telling royalty that you had only found a new land was not good enough. Look at what happened to Raleigh, or to others who disappointed kings in those days; so he called the region the "West Indies." Then the Spaniards called these islands *Las Antillas* from the Portuguese *Antilhas,* similarly pronounced, referring to a legendary set of islands in the far west of the Atlantic. That, too, had no known historical validity, but the name was picked up by the French as *Les Antilles* and the English later identified the *Greater Antilles* and the *Lesser Antilles,* so completing the European authorization of the mistake.

The supposed Caribs were referred to as the (Sp) *Caribes,* (Eng) *Caribees,* and the Spanish *Islas de las Caribes* was translated into English as *Isles of the Caribees,* producing a derivative *Caribbean* (on the pattern of European) referring both to the islands and the mainland home of the Caribs. But today, it is not an exaggeration to say that there are no more Caribs in the Caribbean islands. The only Anglophone territory that warrants the name is in fact Guyana, and the Hispanophone Venezuela, in both of which substantial Carib ethnic groups and clearly accountable Carib languages survive. Moreover, Venezuela has a longer Caribbean seacoast than any of our islands. Trinidad indeed has an ethnic remnant, with a Carib queen, and there are some nonCarib-speaking descendants in St. Vincent and Dominica, but nowhere else in our islands have we got any trace of the Caribs. Carib itself is only one of the six Cariban languages (to use the linguistic label) existing today in Guyana, the other five being Akawaio, Arekuna, Macusi, Patamuna, and Waiwai. Some of these also spread into Venezuela where there are other Cariban languages. Guyana also has two Arawakan languages—Arawak itself, or Lokono, and Wapishana, or Wapichan.

Many loan words, particularly names of timbers, have got into the Guyanese vocabulary from many of these languages and they constitute almost the only actuality there is of what is Carib in our Caribbean "being." So clearly, the term *identity* in our context cannot refer to an ethnicity or nationhood. Still, we must beware of concluding that it is a purely geographical, culturally vague term. At least one contrary reminder exists in the Garifuna of Belize, who are very much more involved as an interactive part of us than are the Caribs of Guyana and Venezuela. The Garifuna are direct descendants of the miscegenation of black Africans and original Caribs of St. Vincent, transplanted to Belize in the eighteenth century; but now, we might note, their identity is so very blurred that they are phenotypically black, though culturally they have their own language and customs.

The third word is *belonging*. I believe many Barbadians do use the notion of "belonging" in a vague way to distinguish the born-and-bred Bajan from all others. In the Bahamas a "belonger" has been identified as "one who has been a known resident of a place for a long number of years although not a native of that place or country." A citation from the *Nassau Tribune* reads:

> Last night's statement by Prime Minister Lynden Pindling now makes it abundantly clear why only a select number of Belongers has been granted citizenship. "This Government," he said, "like any other Government of the day, will decide who are qualified to be citizens at the time their applications come up for scrutiny."[1]

Then there is the term *belongership*, the meaning of which in the Bahamas is indicated in this other citation: "In his affidavit supporting his application, Mr. R—claims that he was granted a Certificate of Belongership on 8 February 1966 for which he paid 50 pounds sterling, and on 20 June 1974, applied to be registered as a Citizen of the Bahamas." So we are getting here a rather specific definition of what it means "to belong" to a Caribbean homeland—and I would say a very narrow, politically administered one whatever its history or rationale. Mind you, the United States and Britain are far worse in this respect; but a political interpretation that would seem holistic for those developed countries could and would readily prove frag-mentive in our multi-ministate context.

How, then, can we define the concept of Caribbean identity? Strevens, a professor of English, finding it impossible to identify the English language in the simple way one could define, say, Norwe-gian as the language of Norway, Danish as the language of the Danes, and so on, ended up in desperation writing the following: "Any piece of human behaviour that is clearly meaningful language whether spoken or written which is not any other language is En-glish."[2] This assertion suggests there is possibly a negative way to tackle our definition problem too. Caribbean identity is instantly de-fined when one is not in the Caribbean. In Brooklyn, in Toronto, in London, in Birmingham, anywhere, one can identify a Caribbean person by his collectively patterned nonmetropolitan speech, man-ner, and lifestyle; but it is principally the pattern of speech that iden-tifies the Caribbean person. I am thinking here, of course, of the Anglophone Caribbean, but probably the same applies to the French Caribbean. For there is a Martinican/Guadeloupean way of speaking that immediately distinguishes them from the metropoli-tan French as *Antillais* (Caribbean), although France fosters a dis-connection of these people from the rest of the Caribbean, main-taining that they are a part of France. Indeed, barriers are emphasized and determined mainly (but we must acknowledge not entirely) in Europe where divisive historical and associated cultural forces are rooted and remain in force. Unfortunately, there is not room here to address this part of our Caribbean identity problem and we must limit ourselves to the Anglophone scene alone.

What identifies the Caribbean or, as they say, West Indian, any-where, is our kind of English, an English with a Caribbean Anglo-phone character—Caribbean English—which when it is heard abroad is clearly not American, not British, not African. It has a dis-tinct type of shift of accent, even when its syntactic structure is what grammarians may call "standard." Its particular combination of pitch and stress (what you might call "accent"), its volume, inten-sity, and accompanying gestures, make our English quite distinctly something that is not anybody else's. That is, in fact, Professor Strev-ens's kind of definition, which I referred to above. But this kind of negative definition clearly will not do. Consider a Swahili proverb introduced to us by Ali Mazrui at the end of his famous television series "The Africans": "The beginning of wisdom is knowing who you are." Now, the Bible says that the beginning of wisdom is the fear of God, but I think the Swahili proverb is better because if you don't know who you are, you couldn't even know that you are a creature of God whom you may then duly fear. So I think the Swahili proverb is a better maxim.

Self-knowledge must begin with our history, and it is right to say we have a common history—essentially, vitally, a history of slavery and our ascendancy therefrom. There has been much persuasion in recent times for us to forget about slavery, the history of which is supposed to be degrading. That is much like saying to a Christian that since Lent and Good Friday are so depressing and degrading, we should think of Easter alone and celebrate only that, like a season without reason.

The English will never forget their Dunkirks and other grim humiliations such as the Battle of the Somme. All nations memorialize their sufferings; one might consider, for example, the Jews. Every year Israelis light a candle in memory of those individuals in the family history who had been in the holocaust, and they let their children light the candles to know and remember that this happened to them as a people. It is a horrible thing to remember, but it gives strength to those people. The horror of our Caribbean ordeal is very real for us too. Though some fifteen decades back in time, it seems to survive in our social consciousness and particularly in our self-destructive attitudes.

Consider, for example, the upset feeling of many members of the Barbadian middle class in regard to the Emancipation Monument, commonly called the Bussa statue. From time to time a letter to the press or even on occasion a public speaker condemns it as an unwanted and degrading monument. But what is the worry about? I am going to suggest that the real horror resides in a kind of collective social aching that stays in our system like a diseased condition whose multiple origins are elusive, perhaps undetected, but covered by mildly euphemistic references to slavery as "dehumanizing," "degrading," and so on. There is also, on occasion, that other popularized claim that East Indian and white indentureship, but particularly East Indian indentureship, was not particularly different from slavery. Well, let us look at the reality evident in a few samples of historical records that will help to rip away both the euphemisms about slavery and by implication the claim of near-sameness of the indentureship system.

The first example is from the *Journal of John Gabriel Stedman*. Stedman was an Englishman sent out to the colony of Surinam as a soldier in the late eighteenth century and, rather unusually for a soldier of his day, he kept a journal of his whole sojourn there for about thirty years. He recorded many of his daily experiences, and I want to present some of his entries:

17 April 1774:
A boy and girl cruelly used by Huysman. A negro infant lately drowned for crying by Mrs. Stoer's own hands. A negro, forced to jump into boiling sugar, who dies, by a Director's cruelty. A negro was lately whipped to death on this plantation.

29 June 1774:
A Jewess out of jealousy murdered a young mulatto girl in a horrid manner by putting a hot iron up her private parts, for which she was sent to the savannah.

14 October 1775:
[He describes a surgeon at the hospital, whose help he was soliciting, but the surgeon was busy in his proper duty, which was the job of amputating limbs from slaves who sought to desert their masters. A leg was taken off for running away, an arm for daring to raise it against a European.] Now this amputation was done by hatchet and all that was done was to tie up the limb so the punished slave wouldn't bleed to death, and could still work.

2 February 1776:
A poor negro woman . . . gets 400 lashes without crying.

20 March 1776:
I dine at Mrs. Godefrooy's. The new raised negroes and mulattoes brought up from Wanica a woman and two children and the hands and ears of several shot bush-negroes.

10 August [1776]:
At Mr. Spaan's house the greatest cruelties happen everyday. I saw, with horror from my window, Miss Spaan give orders that a young black woman should be flogged principally across the breast at which she seemed to enjoy peculiar satisfaction.[3]

Next, let us turn to descriptions in C. L. R. James's *Black Jacobins:*

The torture of the whip, for instance, had "a thousand refinements," but there were regular varieties that had special names, so common were they. When the hands and arms were tied to four posts on the ground, the slave was said to undergo "the four post." If the slave was tied to a ladder it was "the torture of the ladder"; if he was suspended by four limbs it was "the hammock," etc. The pregnant woman was not spared her "four post." A hole was dug in the earth to accommodate the unborn child. The torture of the collar was specially reserved for women who were suspected of abortion, and the collar never left their necks until they had produced a child. The blowing up of a slave had its own name—"to burn a little powder in the arse of a nigger": obviously this was no freak but a recognised practice.[4]

That was eighteenth-century Haiti. Let us travel further up the chain of islands to eighteenth-century Jamaica. Douglas Hall's work, *In Miserable Slavery*, offers us firsthand accounts selected from the diaries of Thomas Thistlewood, an English planter:

> On Wednesday 26 May, the Egypt [the name of the plantation] slaves planted rice in the morass behind the mill house; but that, like much of their others planted, would be eaten by the birds rather than them. And Derby was again catched by Port Royal [another slave] eating canes. I had him well flogged and pickled and then made Hector [that is another slave] shit in his mouth.

> In July, Port Royal, who had run away was taken and brought home. Gave him a moderate whipping, pickled him well, made Hector shit in his mouth, immediately put in a gag, whilst his mouth was full and made him wear it for 4 or 5 hours. Next day, the 24th July, a woman slave, Phillis, caught breaking canes was similarly treated.[5]

This Hector, incidentally, does not escape because he too gets "Derby's dose" on 5 October of the same year. The depravity of this slavemaster is quite unbelievable, but there you have a glimpse of the filthy picture of what happened during plantation slavery.

But barbarity did not cease with slavery, and it is very important to note this. Let me refer you to a text entitled *To Shoot Hard Labour*. It is an account put together from tape recordings made by nine young men of their grandfather's own life story. He lived from 1877 to 1982, 105 years. He was not a slave, nor was his mother. His grandmother was a slave, but he was born out of slavery in 1877, so we are considering a great distance in time from the emancipation year of 1838; we are talking about the postemancipation life of black people in the Anglophone Caribbean, the picture of which is going to be very crucial to our undertanding of why slaves did not go back to the plantations. We have been given to understand that their natural laziness, coupled with the horrible memory of slavery, was enough to keep them away. But we gain further insight from the recorded accounts of Samuel Smith, speaking in his own style of Antiguan creolized English, though it has been edited for the reader's benefit. Although we are more than two generations postemancipation, Smith states:

You was absent from work for whatever reason or late too often, it was jail, or licks, or both. Sometimes after a man did not show up for work his lady friend would take him to massa to be whipped in order for him to get back his job. Many men get whipped that way. It was humiliating, but that's the way it was.

A groom that worked at North Sound Estate for a number of years during my time was one Meryl Jacobs of Potters Village. Suddenly it happened that the estate's calves start to be let loose at nights from time to time and there was no milk the next morning. This gave the planters the suspicion that one of the workers was letting the calves loose. They begin to quietly lie wait at night a little way from the animals and lo and behold, one night they come upon Meryl, the groom, with a bag wrapped around him milking one of them cows. They grab him, tie both hands together, then tie him to the end of the cattle chain. Now we believe them beat he before them tie him to the chain. The cattle dragged Meryl all over the place till morning. When we go to work in the morning, the backra call all the workers to look at Meryl at the end of the cattle chain, with his tongue out of his mouth stiff dead. The planters say he was the scamp. The workers say it was a good thing he got his hands caught in that chain for if not Massa would blame them. The estate provide coffin for Meryl. His people took the body away and that was the end of him. The planters just laugh and say look what happen if you steal. Nobody investigate. In fact nobody die. Meryl was just like a bird or a thing.

The first murder I witness at North Sound was when Harty Babb get killed. Back then [in 1892] the planters use to call the names of the workers each day before the start of work. Our money would be stopped or the backra could take us to the magistrate if we was not present to answer our names. When our names was called we have to answer, "Yes, Massa." One morning after the roll call, we have to wait for orders from the planter in charge of the gang. While we were there waiting, Massa Hinds youngest boy, Ralph, starts to imitate his father and goes calling our names. Everybody answer like usual, until he gets to Harty Babb. At least she didn't answer, "Yes Massa." Now Massa Hinds was close by and he tell her that she was marked absent for not answering. He say she disrespect his son and she was not going to get pay for that day. Then he further accuse her of grumbling bad words at him. In the end he was so annoyed he decide to lash her with a cart whip. When he try this, she resist him, but that didn't last for too long for she was over-powered and he beat her mercilessly. Then he forced her into the estate cellar where he leave her locked up for some days. When he give the order to release her, she was dead. Rats had bitten off her lips and nose. Remember that whatever we have in mind to say to massa about this, we have to keep it to ourselves. If anybody want to cry for Harty, it best to be in quiet or away from the estate. Only women and the small gang workers was seen around the estate that day, for when the news break that Harty Babb dead and have no lips or nose on her face, all the men scamper. They was afraid that the massa would order them in the name of the Queen to take the body out of the cellar. I was at that cellar and saw the body. I'll never forget that day.[6]

What these historical examples point up is fourfold. First, that the brutality of slavemasters was not limited to or worse in any one territory or among this or that European race of masters: whether Dutch, French, or English, Surinam, Haiti, Jamaica, or Antigua, even after emancipation; there are merely variations on the same foul theme. It is, I must stress, idle to believe that what the French did in Haiti they didn't do in Martinique, Guadeloupe, and elsewhere. What is, for instance, the story behind the names of former plantations, in Guyana—Le Repentir (Repentance) and La Penitence (Penitence) just outside Georgetown, left by a French planter. (And the French owned present-day Guyana for only two years, 1782–84.) And idle it would be to believe that Thomas Thistlewood in Jamaica was a unique case of English planters' depravity. It is important to remember, for example, that folk-level Caribbean English vocabulary in many territories contains the word "shit-eater." That "coincidence" tells us something. To believe that such conduct as Thomas Thistlewood's could never have occurred in beautiful Barbados or the magnificent province of Guyana because there is no official record of it is wishful thinking. Thistlewood is a priceless exception to the simple truth that planters would hardly have written up their own heinous acts.

Second, that merely acknowledging slavery was "a horrible, degrading or dehumanizing thing" glosses over unbelievably horrific details which are so painfully hideous a part of Afro-Caribbean ancestral history that some, perhaps many, don't want to know, and would even reject the truth when presented with it. That is exactly the danger in territories such as Guyana and Trinidad now, where East Indian protagonists are strongly asserting that it is they who have earned commanding rights in those countries by supersedence, that is rights of industry and identified Indic culture superseding rights of heritage and a beclouded, unwanted Afric culture.

Third, that any claim or suggestion of indentureship, whether of whites or of the historically more recent and far more numerous East Indians, was hardly different from the slavery of blacks in the Caribbean is a most intolerable exaggeration. Nothing in the closely kept records of indentureship, where every immigrant's name and location was recorded, even remotely approaches the wanton grossness of the accursed practices I have cited—and these citations are only examples. Likening indentureship to slavery, in our Caribbean context is, in my view, an outstanding example of academic dishonesty.

Fourth, that the evidence we have from Antigua provides good reason why emancipated slaves did not go back to the plantations. It wasn't just the grim remembrance of plantation life, but the real danger to life and limb which was exemplified there; and as I indicated above, it would be naive to believe that similar experiences were not to be had in other parts of the Caribbean.

However, more pertinent for us today than the awful reality in the examples and commentary I have given are their consequences for the self-image of Afric Caribbeans. Not only does the collective social memory want to reject the degrading record, but the anxiously preferred alternative of "decency" stimulates an individual fear to identify with public protest of any kind. Thus, for instance, the celebratory character of the Bussa statue in Barbados is seen by many as both degrading and dangerous, a likely cause of bad feeling and undesirable attitudes. But the agonizing fact is that the collective social memory has already enshrined destructive attitudes in the language handed down from way back there in the eighteenth and nineteenth centuries, mentally accepted and *used* by black Caribbeans themselves in our time. Just think, to start with, of some of the idiomatic commonplaces of Caribbean English: *black and ugly, black and stupid, black and ignorant, black and lazy, black and wutliss* [worthless]— as if such pairs belong together like Standard English: *fair and square, good and true,* and so on. Hair is qualified as *bad hair* or *good hair, hard or soft, tough or light, knotty or straight,* and so on. These and many other such terms, and many more linguistically generated concepts persistent in our daily lives, shape the Caribbean identity.

These terms and concepts do not come from the ancestral African languages. They originated here in the Caribbean. Then we get personality adjectives: *stupid, ignorant, nasty, stinking, nigger, t'iefin'.* These labels are part of the spiritual justification of slavery that has been handed to us by the European planter and which have become idiomatically entrenched in our Caribbean identity. *Lazy* is another and particularly interesting term here. The planter was certainly not going to qualify his slaves as lazy, for they were forced to work or die. The label *lazy* would obviously have developed in the postemancipation period as an important part of the justification for the introduction of indentureship. People who did not want to work on plantations, although they would now be paid, must be lazy. Never mind that they were *working* their own *ground.* Never mind the stories like

Samuel Smith's coming from those who did go back. Freed blacks were a lazy bunch, and the vast sugar lands had to be rescued by indentured labor. Simultaneously, there developed a hierarchy of quality identification based on shades of color, black skin marking the embodiment of the basest human qualities labeled as above, with gradations across the spectrum from black to white, identified by a Caribbean vocabulary of adjectives connoting, in the social mind, increasingly better personal qualities: *dark-skinned, clean-skinned, colored, brown-skinned, nice-colored, light brown-skinned, light-skinned, clear-skinned, fair-skinned, cob-skinned, mustee.*

Particularly important to note is that out of the *laziness* syndrome came the belief, widely accepted, that blacks have no staying power. They cannot accomplish ends or maintain positions that require sustained effort: such as a cricket test or series of tests; such as business management; such as the running of a government; such as leadership responsibility for an independent nation, and so on. Even Cheddi Jagan in his book *The West on Trial* manages to qualify the late President Forbes Burnham of Guyana as *lazy.* Jagan states:

> This division was forced upon us for we had soon discovered that Burnham was not one of those who was prepared to undertake arduous work. He had never ventured very far away from Georgetown and had made few contributions to the party newspaper.[7]

Now, whatever bad things one may say about the late Forbes Burnham, he could never be called lazy even by suggestion or implication. On the contrary, the man worked some twenty hours a day, as many fretful spouses of senior civil servants awakened by his 2:00 A.M. telephone calls could attest. But it is not only an ardent debater such as Jagan who is apparently attracted by the facile criticism of laziness in black people, for many Caribbean people also accept it as part of black identity. Even when it is disproved in our own time, as by black Caribbean achievement of success in international cricket, as by the inventiveness shown in the creation of the steel pan (steel drum)—the only new musical instrument of the twentieth century—or by the creative effort of exporting Caribbean Carnival to North America and Britain, and by the thousands of effective educators and administrators and executives that we send to North America, to Britain, and to Africa, the caption of *laziness* sticks to the Caribbean image of the Caribbean black.

It is to be noted, however, that the achievements I have just referred to are all social and cultural products, derived from our roots, and we tend to undervalue their worth and creative power, especially when contrasted with the spectacular achievements of Euro-American science and technology. Self-belittling attitudes undermine our self-confidence and lead to acceptance of white supremacism—that is to say the Euro-American use of mechanical supremacy as a means of control—as an unquestionable given, an illustrated fact of progressive life. Never mind the sustainable liberation to this day of the runaway Maroons of Jamaica or the Bush Negroes of Surinam. Never mind the eighteenth- and early nineteenth-century rebellions that foreran emancipation. Never mind the twentieth-century riots that brought political independence and nationhood all over the Caribbean. These people are lazy! The people whose hands (exclusively) hued down hundreds of square miles of forests, dug hundreds of miles of canals and trenches in Guyana, built property and, in Walter Rodney's words "humanized the land" long before any new immigrant set foot on it, are characterized as "lazy."

Thus, for the makers of that definition, the importation of indentured labor was justified. First came the Portuguese, but they ran away from the field. Not because they were lazy. They just didn't like it. They turned to the easier shop trades. Then came the Chinese, but they ran too, settling for shop-keeping and laundry work. Then came the East Indians in very large numbers and, with operative protection such as the Antiguan freed people would have delighted in, they survived. That they all, Portuguese, Chinese, and East Indian, learned Creole, the territorial dialect of English, from the supposedly lazy, sulking blacks, thus replacing and ultimately all but obliterating the native languages they brought, is an interesting fact telling us that interrelations must have been good and even robust at the outset and for a long time too, for language is not learned in a hostile atmosphere, but rather in peace and friendship. And today the rural East Indian of Guyana and Trinidad is the social maintainer of the most conservative form of the Creoles of those countries.

Yet confrontation, perhaps inevitably in the discriminative framework of white supremacism, did come, and in the context, the idiom of black derogation came in very handy. The established black-and-ugly paradigm was now augmented with the collocation *lazy black* for the convenience of the new population, Portuguese, Chinese, and East Indian, the latter already being familiar with a hierarchy of color brought from their homeland, with a gradation in which the pale-skinned Parsees of northern India were considered socially superior to the darker-skinned Madrasis of the far south. Shiva Naipaul's *Fireflies* has an informative picture of this distinction as still very much operative in present-day Trinidad. The Madrasi mother

of the bride in that novel is recognizably inferior in the East Indian
social hierarchy of the country:

> The bride's mother . . . swept out of our room, flurried but immensely
> happy. "I wonder who she think she is." "I could tell you what she father
> is, darling"; Shantee said, "A low-caste Madrasi cane-cutter."[8]

This is, however, mild when compared with the Indic-Afric confrontation that has developed in Guyana and Trinidad and which, in the
framework of building a unified Caribbean identity, threatens to be
utterly catastrophic.

The natural corollary that seems to follow from a theorem of belief which conflates blackness with laziness is that those who will
work must *belong,* and those who won't work cannot *belong.* Con-
versely, the country properly *belongs* to those who work and not to
those who won't. Hence, the supposed black-and-lazy syndrome becomes a serious political issue: you can forget about the history of
black rebellions that first forced freedom on the Caribbeanwide
lands; you can forget about the survival labors of the Maroons that
gave an extra meaning to the Caribbean word *maroon,* that of "coop-
erative labor," spawning many others with similar meaning throughout the Caribbean to this very day: *lend-hand* (Tobago); *diggings,
morning-work, pardner* (Jamaica); *kiap* (Guyana); *koudmen* (*coup-de-
main*) (Dominica, St. Lucia), etc. You can forget, too, about the collective sweat-labors of postemancipation blacks that, all over the Caribbean, built villages whose names tell a tale. I know many in Guyana, such as Now-or-Never, Liberty, Two Friends, Three Friends,
Friendship, Sisters, Endeavor, etc. Finally, you can forget about the
pre-World War II, black and bloody, regional riots that brought out
the Royal Commission of 1938, through which came the pioneer
University of the West Indies in 1948 and independent nationhood
for some twelve Caribbean states in the 1960s and 1970s. All that
muscle and mind belong merely to history, and so too does heritage.
Or does it?

Interestingly, for example, the national anthem of Barbados has
these lines:

> Our brave forefathers sowed the seed
> From which our pride is sprung.
> A pride that makes no wanton boast
> Of what it has withstood . . .

and its chorus asserts

We loyal sons and daughters all
Do hereby make it known
These fields and hills beyond recall
Are now our very own.

And the second verse ends: "And greater will our nation grow in strength and unity."

Now the question must be asked, Are Caribbean blacks with the same history entitled to the same sentiments anywhere in the Caribbean? Perhaps. But only perhaps, for the case of Guyana illustrates that, by the ground rules of democracy, the grand sentiments of the Barbados national anthem may not be relevant, for these ground rules take no account of history, heritage, or culture. They require that a statistical majority, established on a chosen day, shall determine who makes the rules of ownership and control of the country thereafter. If that statistical majority turns out to be a nonintegrative, race-conscious grouping of East Indians, as happens to be largely the case in Guyana today, then it is they who will decide what constitutes ownership. The same question has begun to be put if perhaps less poignantly in Trinidad, but Guyana is the most poignant and a sufficient example of the issue.

However, there are many more serious questions. Why must the issue in Guyana or Trinidad be one born of the politics of racial division? Do East Indians, Hindu and Muslim, really group racially? Is the Indic policy of nonintegration based on religious or other tenets? Why can't national issues encourage and foster integration as the best way to tackle the nation's problems? Are black claims, based on history, heritage, and culture, really sure? That is, are blacks sure of their culture, as East Indians seem to be sure of theirs? Whatever the answer, must such differences of culture or of attitudes make a unified Caribbean identity undependable? There are also other questions. Hasn't each race contributed significantly to the socio-economic substance of Guyana and of Trinidad? Can't Indic and Afric *belongers* be realistic marriage partners in the same domestic households? and so on. Clearly, such are matters for inspection, investigation, and discussion, with the gravest rationality.

How difficult this is going to be is readily demonstrated by the situation, typically observed, whenever an Indian or Pakistani cricket team comes to the West Indies to play against the West Indies team. Consider, for example, an advertisement placed in the *Barbados Nation* newspaper of 8 April 1989 by members of the Indian community on behalf of their businesses:

We welcome the Indian cricket team to Barbados and wish them success in the Second Test Match. Good luck from the following stores, members of the Indian Community of Barbados.[9]

The advertisement goes on to list the several participating stores. Clearly, there is confusion here. One must ask, Who are the "We"? Are they really West Indians? Are they not Barbadians? Are they just paranational money makers? Quite apart from what may be seen as the outrageousness of such a statement of position, it would seem to me to be the duty of the general Barbadian community to discuss through the press the issue of nationhood and loyalty with the protagonists of such opinions. But that was never done, and if the people don't assault such divisive attitudes, politicians never will. For, clearly, politicians operate and many thrive only on division, on opposing parties and nowadays even on party paramountcy. We must turn for help to social thinkers and to academics of all races. But we may find ourselves in difficulties there too.

For instance, it is disturbing that in his preface to *India in the Caribbean* David Dabydeen of Warwick University makes the following claim:

Indians have been able to make significant, sometimes unique contributions on every level of Caribbean activity, in spite of the injustice and violence they endured. Their peasant agricultural skills for instance fed, and still feed, Guyana. In the realm of politics, leaders of Indian origin like Cheddi Jagan, spearheaded the Caribbean movement towards independence and became world figures as a result of their agitation.[10]

The claim regarding Jagan is simply untrue and grossly misleading. Jagan had not even entered the political arena when T. A. Marryshow of Grenada, Norman Manley of Jamaica, Eric Williams of Trinidad, and Grantley Adams of Barbados really "spearheaded" moves for universal adult suffrage, self-government, and federation—all of which were the realistic and obvious stages toward independence, starting with self-government for Jamaica in 1944, and Marryshow's push for a Federation as early as 1946.[11] However, such claims are not limited to the editorial commentary of Dabydeen and Samaroo in their text, *India in the Caribbean*. In the opening lecture of the University of the West Indies "Humanities Festival," George Lamming,[12] perhaps the doyen of our Caribbean social analysts, made a statement in a part of his address which prompted the following headline in the *Barbados Advocate*:

LAMMING: CARIBBEAN CULTURE BASED ON INDIAN LABOUR

The report begins: "Noted West Indian author, Dr. George Lamming says that Caribbean culture is based on Indian labour . . ." etc.[13]

The actual text of Dr. Lamming's statement reads:

If labour is the foundation of all culture, then the Indian presence in Trinidad was part of the very first floor on which that house was built. This concept of labour, fundamental to all of my thinking, this concept of labour and the relations experienced in the process of labour is the foundation of all culture, and this is crucial to what I mean by the Indian presence as a creative Caribbean reality. For it is through work that men and women make nature a part of their own history. *The way we see, the way we hear, our nurtured sense of touch and smell, the whole complex of feelings which we call sensibility is influenced by the particular features of the landscape which has been humanized by our work, so that there can be no history of Trinidad or Guyana that is not also a history of the humanization of those landscapes by Indian and other human forces of labour.* (The emphases are mine.)[14]

The statement, you will note, does not limit itself to the case for the proper consideration of the Indian as part of the Caribbean reality. It moves him from being "a part of the very first floor" of Caribbean culture to the forefront, that is, "Indian and other" of the human forces of labor that effected "humanization of those landscapes" of Trinidad and Guyana. Such is not only a questionably high claim. It must be set against what Dr. Lamming had previously stated elsewhere, as for example, in the foreword to Walter Rodney's *History of the Guyanese Working People: 1881–1905*:

The point Rodney wants to be remembered is the means whereby such labour [the digging of drainage canals] was undertaken. This meant that slaves moved 100 million tons of heavy water-logged clay with shovel in hand, while enduring conditions of perpetual mud and water . . . Working people continued making a tremendous contribution to the *humanization* of the Guyanese coastal landscape.[15]

It is the operative word, *humanization*, that confirms his real intention. Such an emphasis leads to an overwhelming conclusion. The history of humanization of that landscape is primarily the history of those hands. And Lamming goes on in several paragraphs to describe how the brutal challenge of the sea to that Guyanese coastal landscape necessitated the work of the Sea Defence, which persists to this day.

It is important to recall that Guyana's coast is the victim of an erosion cycle and there is a time when the tides of the Atlantic turn and, with the outflow of the Amazon, do a dreadful job of pulling away the shore mud of the whole coastline. The Dutch built the "sea wall," for which Georgetown is famous, as part of what has become a long-term job known as the *Sea Defence*. The Guyana coastline is supposed to be six feet below sea level, so when the fury of the sea is at its worst, work goes on through the day and night driving piles, bringing mud and piling it up to prevent the sea from coming further inland. At the turn of the century and during the first decades of the twentieth, this was well known to be the task of black labor. The East Indians were on the plantations where they were employed to plant sugar. But the black descendants of freed men had villages to maintain in the backlands; and those villages were going to be flooded with salt water if they didn't work day and night to keep the sea out. These were the same lazy fellows, along the East Coast of Demerara, who drove piles, built dams, burned earth, and lifted stones to counterattack the sea's erosion, while the East Indians were on the sugar plantations as plantation labor.

I can only conclude that Lamming's shock in discovering, with warm and deserved respect, the humble, early morning East Indian hawkers in Trinidad—such being his first experience of colonialized folk culture outside of his native Barbados[16]—led him to forget not only his own compatriot black Barbadian hawkers trekking to Bridgetown at three and four o'clock in the morning in order to feed the middle class in Barbados, but also the early morning higglers of Louise Bennett's verses and Stella's "Party Line," who were feeding Kingston, Jamaica; the Guyanese hucksters, mostly black, who have set up the parallel market between the Caribbean islands and Georgetown in order to beat the absurdities of the present-day Guyanese domestic economy; the pork knockers who produce or perish in the roughest of individual gold-mining ventures in Guyana's dense interior; the dock workers, the coastal fishermen and women, the schooner trade seafarers—all black labor, and sometimes black enterprise as well. Are all these just "other human forces" superseded by East Indian labor in the *humanization* of the Caribbean landscape, or even, if we wish to limit the scene, the Guyanese and Trinidadian landscapes?

Clearly, what we need to do, in place of making or countering emotive claims with destructively explosive potential, is to seek to build that framework for productive cultural meld, a synthesis through cross-fertilization which, as I stated above, politics will not help us to do. For whether or not one accepts, with Lamming, that "labour is the foundation of all culture," it is indisputable that culture is the foundation of all nation-building. If Caribbean identity is to be established, and is to create and produce to advance us all, then we must take due account of all aspects of its mosaic, big pieces and small, multicolored and many-shaded. Perhaps as many Caribbeans see and feel this need as those who do not. It is the vital role of the intellectual to make most Caribbeans want it and move to make it so. To do otherwise is to head straight for disaster in its most dread form, and this is not an exaggeration. Several areas of the world at this very moment demonstrate the gruesome option which we have all been challenged to inspect.

Briefly look, for example, at Canada which, having failed to address cultural integration of the Francophone and Anglophone divisions in its culture as a vital necessity, now has its nationhood and economy arguably hamstrung by that error. Notwithstanding highly developed science and national technology and great business power, Canada is hamstrung. But this is only an example of unintegrated cultures throttling national economic development, and thus it might be seen by some as a mild case of the problem I have been discussing.

Look then at the technologically fearsome USSR which used military might to smother cultural divisions, so it believed; yet the Union is now irrevocably torn asunder by those very cultural divisions, some twenty of them, the split begun by pugnacious little Estonia, Latvia, and Lithuania, three tiny countries, three little frost-bitten Davids that got together and told the Soviet Goliath to go to hell. They started the crack and then the rest of the USSR went asunder. In each case, there was a culture solid enough to be identified by its own language and literature, whether large (Ukrainian) or small (Estonian)—quite distinct from Muscovite Russian. Now we can see the result of the great USSR's failure to underpin its military and technological prowess by respecting and embracing the cultural souls of its many different peoples. In spite of the nationalizing force of pride in the former Soviet Union's spectacular technology—first satellite in space and all that—they are now "catspraddled," as many of us Caribbeans say, sprawled apart for want of that adhesive strength which only a melded and ultimately welded culture can provide.

Lastly, consider the horror of the former Yugoslavia: Muslim, Serb, and Croat within one "nation" trapped in internecine slaughter. Thirty thousand women multi-gang-raped until their pregnancy was ensured. This is only one example of the dread disaster, the gruesome option I mentioned above. Religion and ethnicity are among the deadliest "volcanic" mixtures any nation has to fear, and we are walking right into that mixture in the southern Caribbean if we don't tackle the need to build an integrated, regional under-standing and an anxious mutual respect through studying who we Caribbeans are. In Warwick (England), in Berlin, Vienna, and Utrecht (Europe), and in Gainesville (Florida, U.S.A.) there are Centres for Caribbean Studies and Research. There is also an Insti-tute of Caribbean Studies at the University of Puerto Rico, but there is no such organized institute in our own University of the West In-dies. We need to address this most urgently, yet we have not properly begun, while others located elsewhere have done so.

An Institute of Caribbean Studies should have large branches in the campus territories of the University of the West Indies and in Guyana, as well as small branches attached to relevant institutions in every other Caribbean territory. It should study language, as basic to our understanding of each other, not just lingusitics and the use of English, but the conceptual structure of the languages of the African diaspora, relevant Indic languages, the Amerindian languages of Guyana, the Chinese and Portuguese cultural imports, and espe-cially Afric and Indic cultural imports. It should focus especially on the cultural equations of Caribbean and South American Spanish, Brazilian Portuguese, Caribbean French, and our own Caribbean English. This can be profitably pursued in two scholarly ways: a) through the study of parallel or comparable human experiences as reflected in our literatures, and b) through the study of the region-alization of the metropolitan languages, whether as Creoles, or as creolized or formal varieties.

In addition, it should investigate a Caribbean theology, a huge and difficult subject being tentatively broached by individuals such as Father Harcourt Blackett, the Reverend Kortright Davis, and oth-ers. Relatively recently, there was the formation of the Barbados Inter-Religious Organisation (BIRO). We must take further steps like that, inviting the Hindu, the Muslim, the Baha'i, the Christian, the Rastafarian to think and talk together about the oneness of God, putting behind what Europe has done to us, and putting before the astonishing advantage of being thrown together by a strange Provi-dence—from China, India, Indonesia, Africa, Europe, and Native America (the so-called Amerindian). Nowhere else in the world has such an interracial phenomenon occurred. But it seems clear that European Christianity cannot solve our problems. Are the Chris-tians going to tell the Hindus of Guyana that if they become Chris-tians all will be well? That is next to nonsense. Indeed, Christianity, trammeled by its European heritage of exclusiveness, domination, hierarchy, expensive edifices, lifeless denominational routines, etc., is often much more of a divisive than an integrative force. Instead we need to seek the method and means to put together complementary beliefs which operate on the transreligious commandment "to love one's neighbor as oneself" and seek interracial Caribbean brotherhood through that route. All that may seem too much to ask of an Institute of Caribbean Studies, but we can at least ask that the subject of a Caribbean theology be broached.

But there are certainly less taxing and more readily achievable goals that an Institute of Caribbean Studies could set itself. For instance, are the practices of unionism adopted from Europe and carrying the hallmark of the International Labor Organization still the best for maximum profitability, productivity, and competitive trading in and by our Caribbean peoples? What about *cooperativism*, a word and concept coming from Guyana, or a participatory labor-and-proprietor ownership which could serve to make strikes irrelevant? An Insititute of Caribbean Studies could help to make tourism a popular, participatory exercise practiced by an enlightened population, rather than a product fundamentally dictated by the modalities of external markets.

An Institute of Caribbean Studies, preferably independent of the University of the West Indies, but whether so or not, could authorize its own certification. The UWI typically baulks at issuing certificates except for degrees or diplomas, at one time even refusing certification for attendance at accredited extramural courses. If certification of even a minor worthwhile achievement is an effective incentive to achieve, then let the piece of paper, duly logographed, be offered, *earned*, and awarded. I am sure that certificates with distinction grades for hair braiding, stage dancing, creole cooking, kitchen gardening, etc., would bring a lot of pride, industry, and cash.

I wish to conclude this essay with what I call the three Caribbean "R"s: Reggae, Road March, and Rum. Briefly put, reggae has not only become a Caribbean institution, it has been internationalized, and Jamaica has accepted an Institute of Reggae Studies as an objective. Japan has taken to reggae as well, with young Japanese admirers even adopting the Rastafari hairstyle. What we are witnessing is simply the high international saleability of our Caribbean culture which our own governments seem unwilling to recognize in any intelligently promotive way.

The next "R" for Road March I am actually using to draw our attention to the steel pan. As I stated above, the steel pan is the only new musical instrument invented in the twentieth century. It seems as though that thought only struck some of us recently, although the invention took place in Trinidad in the 1940s. Indeed, I believe it is only now beginning to dawn on the engineering department of the University of the West Indies that the steel pans could be scientifically produced, pressed out from machine-operated moulds, subjected to acoustic studies and tuned by the ears of experts, just as manufactured grand-piano strings are fashioned in European and Japanese factories. Already the Japanese have begun to do as much with the steel pan. After all, there is no international patent for it and so I have little doubt that the day is not far off when perhaps we shall have Yamaha steel pans imported from Japan, for sale throughout the Caribbean, including Trinidad where they were invented.

The final "R" is for Rum. When the African, Caribbean, and Pacific association of nations met with the European Economic Commission in Barbados in January, 1989 to prepare the LOME IV agreement,[17] France, a powerful member of that body, proposed a redefinition of rum. If France's redefinition had been accepted, it would have made rum an agricultural rather than an industrial product. The whole aim and effect of such a redefinition would have been to make only the heavy, dark rums of Martinique, Guadeloupe, and the French-affiliated African countries recognizable commercially as rums, while all the light rums and white rums of Guyana, Trinidad, Barbados, Jamaica, indeed the whole Anglophone Caribbean as well as Cuba, would have become ineligible for commercial recognition as rums in Europe. This would have meant the loss of millions of dollars in rum sales in Europe for these Caribbean member countries, with equivalent millions in gain for the French affiliates. Here were the French delegates boldly disputing the right to the name *rum* in its own Caribbean home base.

This French attack, for it was no less than that, took the Caribbean contingent by surprise. Perhaps in desperation, the then Minister of Trade and Industry of Barbados and his permanent secretary approached me, as a result of my work in Caribbean lexicography, for a just definition of rum. I referred them to Richard Ligon's *A True and Exact History of the Island of Barbados* where, with carefully detailed drawings, the industrial production of rum is indisputably demonstrated; but better still, it is made clear that the liquor, at first called *kill-devil*, was produced by a succession of boiling processes which ultimately prompted the name *rum-bullion*, a slang name meaning "fine (boiled) drink."[18]

Thereafter it was only a matter of time before the immensely popular drink was fondly pet-named *rum* by sailors and soldiers. In just the same way, that is to say by reduction of syllables, seasoned drinkers had pet-named *brandewine* ("burnt wine") *brandy, whiskebaugh* ("water of life") *whiskey, genever* (one of its ingredients) *gin,* etc. But what is vital to us here is that its world popularity stems from a history which firmly places both the product rum and its name in Barbados. When a definition duly conceived from the cultural information that I had supplied was offered to the French EEC contingent (a definition backed up by the evidence of the famous French etymologist Albert Dauzat's *Dictionnaire etymologique* that *rum* is "un mot des iles Barbades"), their commercial attack collapsed, and Caribbean rum won the day. It meant millions to us in exports and in jobs.

These few examples ought to suggest to us the value and importance of Caribbean cultural identity and the vital necessity of truly knowing our cultural history. This deep historical and cultural knowing is fundamental to that process of identity. And where, let us remember, did the huge cash value of these Caribbean successes, as in reggae, the steel pan, and rum come from? From the history and roots of the culture of our Caribbean identity. Are we wise to all this, or are we so dazzled by the technology of the North that we are ignoring the very real, very tangible value of the wisdom grown by our own culture? The beginning of that wisdom is, as the profound African proverb tells us, *knowing who we are!*

Notes

1. See the *Nassau Tribune,* 11 January 1975, 1.

2. Strevens, "Varieties of English," *English Studies* 45 (1964): 164.

3. *Journal of John Gabriel Stedman 1744–1797,* ed. S. Thompson (London, 1962).

4. C. L. R. James, *The Black Jacobins* (New York: Random House, 1963), 13.

5. Douglas Hall, *In Miserable Slavery: Thomas Thistlewood in Jamaica, 1750–86* (London: Macmillan, 1989), 72.

6. Keithlyn and Fernando Smith, *To Shoot Hard Labour: The Life and Times of Samuel Smith, An Antiguan Workingman, 1877–1982* (Scarborough, Ontario: Edan Press, 1986), 81, 75–76, 73–74.

7. Cheddi Jagan, *The West on Trial* (London: Michael Joseph, 1966), 112.

8. Shiva Naipaul, *Fireflies* (Harmondsworth: Penguin Books, 1970), 197.

9. Advertisement, *Barbados Nation,* 8 April 1989, 2.

10. David Dabydeen and Brinsley Samaroo, eds., *India in the Caribbean* (London: Hansib, 1987), preface.

11. See Jill Sheppard, *Marryshow of Grenada: An Introduction* (Barbados: Letchworth Press, 1989), chap. 6.

12. The lecture, entitled "Caribbean Labour, Culture and Identity," was delivered by Dr. Lamming on 6 March 1994 at the Cave Hill campus of the University of the West Indies. See note 16.

13. *Barbados Advocate,* 11 March 1994, 4.

14. I am grateful to Glyne Griffith for allowing me to peruse the relevant pages of George Lamming's address for the purpose of the present essay.

15. See George Lamming, foreword to Walter Rodney, *History of the Guyanese Working People: 1881–1905* (London: Heinemann, 1981), xviii.

16. See the full text of Lamming's address in this issue of the *Bucknell Review.*

17. The African, Caribbean, and Pacific (ACP) association of nations meets with the European Economic Commission (EEC) every four or five years to review aid and trade agreements. The site of the first such meeting, Lome, the capital city of Togo, gave its name to the series of meetings.

18. Richard Ligon, *A True and Exact History of the Island of Barbados* (London: Parker, 1657), 84. And here we also have the evidence of the *Oxford English Dictionary,* vol. 8.

Calypso and Caribbean Identity

Gordon Rohlehr

University of the West Indies, St. Augustine, Trinidad

T HERE are many ways in which one could interpret the topic, "Calypso and Caribbean Identity." For example, one could ask, What does one learn through the study of the calypso about the nature of the Caribbean experience and the kinds of people that the Caribbean has produced? The ready answer of course is that one can learn a great deal, because the calypso covers so many aspects of life. Some may say that at times it covers these aspects superficially, but there are many calypsos which cover them with a great degree of penetration and sophistication. Just recently, for example, there was a book of discography published on the Mighty Sparrow's calypsos and part of that discography carefully categorized Sparrow's recorded calypsos (and here you're talking about 79 or so LPs) into themes, and I counted over 350 themes. Therefore, if the work of a single singer, granted a fairly monumental sort of singer, can be broken down into so many themes (and I'm sure that there are more to be found if one carefully scrutinizes Sparrow's work), then the thematic approach could easily yield a very lengthy discourse on calypso and Caribbean identity.

An alternative approach would be to select a body of calypsos from throughout the region which has dealt directly with the theme of Caribbean identity—there are one or two calypsos published every year on Caribbean identity—and perhaps we could compare the ideas which emerge from these. This second approach I will not explore here. Because my data at present is confined to the calypsos of Trinidad and Tobago, I will confine my discussion to these calypsos only. Indeed, relatively few calypsos from outside Trinidad and Tobago ever become popular in the twin-island state, which might tell us something about Caribbean identity too. Although we are relatively close to each other geographically, somehow exchanges which should take place between and among us do not take place.

Thus, only the singers themselves often know of many of these songs as a result of their travel to places like Brooklyn or Miami, which is where they meet each other. These places are, in fact, the unofficial capitals of the Caribbean and can be understood to represent an unacknowledged Caribbean federation.

In places such as Miami or New York or Washington D.C. where there are transplanted Caribbean communities you get someone such as radio personality Von Martin in Washington D.C. doing a four-hour program every Saturday afternoon on the Caribbean. Martin, for example, presents a program which cuts across the Caribbean, offering news and music from the Caribbean region; that is then juxtaposed to an African program, and so on. Thus, in those metropolitan centers, somehow we find a wider variety of the Caribbean identity. The Caribbean peoples are juxtaposed to each other more closely in diaspora contexts than they are in actuality in the Caribbean regional setting. It may be our contemporary way of doing what we used to do in the colonial period, that is, to relate more closely as Caribbean peoples living in "exile" in another country than we relate to each other back "home" in the Caribbean. And the country outside the region which we Caribbean peoples now generally relate to is more likely to be America than Great Britain. So, let us consider option number one, that is, through a study of the calypso, what are some of the things one might learn about the nature of the Caribbean experience and the kinds of people the Caribbean has produced? Moreover, let us begin to do so even with this terrible awareness of the problem of trying to define or speak meaningfully about Caribbean identity.

What ways of defining identity can we adopt? For example, one might say that a person's identity is what the person is as an individual in the privacy of his or her soul. I don't know whether we can learn very much about this through the calypso, since at present we're not certain how many calypsonians actually write their own calypsos. This matter is further complicated when one considers the significant number of female calypsonians there are now who are singing some powerfully feminist songs, all written by men. So the question of looking at who the person is in the privacy of his or her soul is a tricky one in terms of the calypso. A second approach might be to view the individual Caribbean identity as a product or a construct of a particular process of socialization, and I think one can learn a great deal about that sort of thing from the calypso. Then, there is the question of the person within the ethnos, the influence and relevance of the ethnic identity as fundamental to any understanding of Caribbean identity. This is often a privileged theme in calypso, especially in the Trinidadian context. There is, again, the question of national identity as against regional identity, and there is also gender identity, all of which in some quarters are represented as mutually exclusive modes of identity in constant confrontation with each other or fumbling toward some kind of dialogue of mutual understanding. These, then, are some of the ways that people group themselves together and exercise loyalties, and Caribbean identity might involve some or all of these modes of comprehending Caribbean selfhood. Thus the grand question becomes, How does one understand a Caribbean and define a Caribbean identity in a region that is multiethnic, multilingual, multicultural, and ideologically plural?

In Trinidad and Tobago, there is the recurrent question, particularly these days, as to whose culture should have prominence. There is what you might call "competitive ethnicity," which we have had in a country such as Guyana for a long time. There is a struggle for visibility, for tangible recognition in terms of state and private funding, promotion, and acceptance in the eyes of the others. Whenever we talk about culture, that kind of struggle is taking place. Then there are divisions within particular territories, and these divisions mean that questions of national self-definition are nowhere being solved, let alone questions of regional self-definition. Current cultural theory tends to recognize the right to difference, the right of autonomy of even the smallest cultural grouping, and the urge to celebrate the uniqueness of numerous individual cultures. How such differences ought to relate to each other and to overarching national objectives is by no means clear. Do such differences, for example, make the individual nation more exploitable and prone to manipulation from outside since there is no common core of values, no core of national identity?

One might compare the history of ethnic struggle in Trinidad to something like an American football game, that game where two sides batter each other to gain ten yards of space. They move forward, then they move backward, and then it seems they move sideways, and despite all the battering it can be quite some time before they move anywhere at all. They bruise ribs, they gouge eyes, they jump on each other, and so on, and meanwhile somebody else is up there controlling the show, raking in the spoils. It is never the players, really. No matter what they gain or think they have gained, there are others who benefit even more as a result of the orchestrated battering on the field and that's what happens with these sorts of ethnic struggles in a small Caribbean space. The country itself becomes more exploitable, but you can't tell any of the groups of people not to express their ethnic desires, not to define themselves in this or that way.

How then might we move from these unresolved and perhaps unresolvable differences within individual Caribbean territories to what is an even loftier desire, a Caribbean community? Would we even be talking about the Caribbean community these days were we not threatened collectively by the now monolithic world order of globalization? Would we be engaging in these discussions with such renewed fervor were we not being threatened with national and cultural suffocation and possible extinction? I don't think it is easy to extinguish us, but I do think that a monolithic globalization is likely to give it a good try. How then does the calypso relate to all of these questions so that you can see how complex and pertinent these issues are or can be?

Let us begin by approaching the question of multiethnicity. Some years ago, a research student of mine at the St. Augustine campus of the University of the West Indies wrote a paper on race and color in preindependent Trinidadian literature. The student ended up by recognizing that this fiction was being written by peoples of different ethnicities. There was, for example, Seepersad Naipaul, Alfred Mendes, and C. L. R. James, among others. Through the fiction one was able to discern various ethnic perspectives and concerns within the Trinidadian complex, and within these narratives the reader was provided with a spectrum of ethnic possiblities. But what the research student discovered was that in terms of the representation of major characters and ethnocultural experiences and perspectives within the Trinidadian context but outside their own ethnic milieu, many of these writers seemed unable to transcend the stereotypical ethnic perceptions and sensibilities of their own particular group. In other words, they never put somebody from an ethnic group different from their own at the center of their fictions, or if on occasion they did, these characters tended to remain stereotypical constructions of ethnic groups as viewed from outside the group. These narrative "others" were almost always presented at the periphery and, as indicated above, tended to be seen only in terms of stereotypes.

If we look at calypsos that try to address these problems, we might usefully begin with the recognition that the calypso itself is a product of processes originating in various cultures and evolving out of various ethnic groups or ethnic communities. Its entire history has been one of a certain degree of multiethnicity and it has therefore developed flexibility and is constantly, of course, undergoing change. Thus, in the calypso, today's innovation soon becomes tomorrow's tradition; indeed this is in keeping with the very nature of the calypso. If we look at the origins of the calypso as music, we will get a sense of the complexity of Caribbean identity.

There are several theories about this origin. One of these is that the calypso is a continuation of African musics in a Caribbean situation, evolving from the social reality of slave-plantation practice where several African nations were forced to intermix and in the process merged their respective traditions of melody, rhythm, and origin. A second theory is that the birth and development of calypso is a direct or indirect transference of European troubadorian practice in the context of French Creole, nineteenth-century Trinidad. African slaves or freed men, this theory argues, learned the troubadorian practice from their masters. The third position contends that the calypso is a product of the appropriation by Africans of the music of the decimated, indigenous peoples, the Caribs of Trinidad. There is not too much evidence for this third position since nobody really knows much about the nature and type of music produced by the Caribs of Trinidad, but the hypothesis exists nonetheless. Fourth, there is the argument that the calypso is the result of appropriation by Africans of the various musics to which they were exposed in an ethnically diverse society that would have included French Creoles, Spanish Creoles, various classes of British, other West Indians, various nations of Africa and later, Portuguese, Indians, Chinese, and other Asiatics. Thus you begin to glimpse the problem of Caribbean identity in just one place, Trinidad, and in just one musical form, the calypso.

My own approach to the idea of the origin of the calypso blends the first and fourth theories. It assumes and recognizes from evidence that may be gleaned from all over the Antilles and indeed from those societies in South and North America to which Africans had been transported, that Africans took their musics with them wherever they went. It assumes, too, that these musics supplied a solid core of melodies and rhythms and fulfilled a variety of functions that have not really changed throughout the centuries. Among the functions fulfilled by African musics are first of all, worship, giving thanks and praise to the great spirit of life through song and dance. This has been a major function of African music.

Worship expressed in the musical idiom may contain a mixture of awe, dread, fear, love, and affirmation, and generally involves an invocation of the powers or energies associated with deity. It sustains a dimension of the sacred which has survived consistent attempts by the plantation owners, the established Christian churches, and the imperial law to abolish African worship in the Antilles. The calypso as an evolving musical idiom employed Orisha chants taken out of their context and set to different drum rhythms, and this experiment may have provided the basis for the minor-key melodies of the stick-fighting songs. There was a convincing presentation on this topic by professor Maureen Warner Lewis, who conducted her study on Yoruba culture and linguistic retention in Trinidad.[1] She collected some 150 Yoruba songs and took them back with her to Nigeria, learnt some Yoruba herself and got translations so that she was able to relocate these songs in their original cultural contexts and discuss them with a greater degree of authority. The point to be made here is that if you take some of those Yoruba melodies and set them to a beat and slow them down somewhat, you get some of those minor-key melodies reminiscent of the early minor-key calypso chants. They may not have been derived only from these Yoruba origins, but they very probably did originate there. You certainly find that sort of assimilation taking place.

The second function is that of the battle chant, songs for war and confrontation. The stick fight was a martial art. The stick fight, for me, is one of the most appropriate metaphors for understanding Trinidadian society. I think everything that takes place in the social and cultural contexts in Trinidad possesses some element of conflict and is reminiscent of a stick fight. This sort of situation occurs all the time in calypsos of all sorts. The stick fight had its own music and that music had a distinct structure which became the foundation of what later came to be known as the calypso. That structure in the calypso was the fundamental structure of a wide variety of African musics of the so-called call and response, or litany, form. Such a structure usually involves an intimate exchange between a lead singer and a chorus. This exchange is itself symbolic of the interplay between the individual and the group, whether the group be clan, nation, village, family, a work group such as the Haitian *coumbite*, the Arawak, Hispanic, or African *gayape*, the Tobago *lend-hand*, or other aggregations of miscellaneous folk culture and situation, such as the *yards* of Georgetown, Kingston, Port of Spain, or Tiger Bay, the so-called ghettos, renamed by insightful, expressive folk vernacular as observed in examples such as "The Dungle," "Hell-Yard," or "Back-O-Wall."

Africans reconstructed New World versions of their lost and shattered kindred, and these versions were reflected in the musical structures of their religious liturgies, their war songs, their work songs, and their songs of celebration. Many of their songs would have blended all of these modes, worship, battle, work, and celebration. You can probably find elements of all of these happening in the same musical structure. Now this might not seem to some like calypso and Caribbean identity, but I am insisting that it is. I am insisting that in looking at the origin and the structure of the music, we are looking in fact at the deep structure, a linguistic term, of Caribbean society and identity. That is where we really get to the foundations of Caribbean identity, the deep structure which lies underneath, so that the question of call and response, the question of the *kalinda*, or war song, the question of conflict, is indeed a central question of Caribbean identity, and it grows naturally out of the nature of the multiethnic community which is Caribbean reality.

African communities on the Continent were and are multiethnic, and they had their disagreements and disputes among themselves. Among these communities, for example, the Congolese were reputed to be magicians, and they were feared because it was thought that they could work *obeah* or *voodoo* and this kind of thing. The Yoruba were known to be very good at *picong*, that very sharp sarcasm born of a keen wit and a facility with the pun. And so you had a kind of *jamming*, a repartie which was deeply structured in the society and which is part of the calypso and Caribbean popular culture even today. One was always dealing with conflict, and the calypso has always registered this fact.

The third function is the function of work, and the practice of the work song was and still is African. I am not saying that only African peoples sing work songs. I am simply establishing that Africans came to the plantation slavery of the New World with their music and did not stop singing merely because they had become enslaved. In fact, they sang even more because they had become enslaved. They may have sung with a fiercer intensity since it is well known that the music of the New World diaspora Africans was often a vehicle for subversion. It was employed to pass on messages secretly. There is, for example, a text, *Black Song: The Forge and the Flame* by John Lovell, and in this work Lovell writes about the spirituals evolving out of the American plantation system, and he addresses the ways in which these songs functioned as a means of transmitting messages about the underground railroad and the plans which people made to escape slavery.[2] Hence, *Zion* and *Jordan*, for example, are still code names for those regions of freedom and grace beyond the confines of the oppressive system which the Rastafarians term *Babylon*. The Rastafarians incorporated these terms in the Caribbean context, but the same terminology had been used to represent part of a whole system of subversion and escape throughout plantation America.

The structure of the work song was no different from that of the war song; it, too, was built on call and response, although its rhythm would change according to the type of work which was being done.

So if you were digging or hauling or hammering, you would have a different kind of song or chant. If, for example, you were digging, you might chant: "Woman ah heavy load," and everybody would respond: "Uh huh!" That "Uh huh" locates the moment when you transmit maximum energy into whatever implement you're using—pickaxe, pitchfork, hammer, or whatever. The strategy connects the pattern of breathing with an efficient means of transmitting and focusing energy, and these transplanted Africans employed their version of this, which is why they sang when they worked, and they had particular rhythms for particular situations. What is particularly noticeable in all of these types of songs is that the form was determined by the function. If, for example, the required objective was to get twenty workers to strike the soil with their hoes at the same time, then the form of the music would contain both verbal and rhythmic signals which would convey to the workers the precise moment to strike the soil. In addition, the beat of the hoe, hammer, pitchfork, or pickaxe would, in its turn, contribute to and form part of the rhythm of the song. Indeed, all of this is at once simple and complex. That is to say, this galvanizing of a group of people around some basic rhythm in which communal energy is simultaneously expended toward the fulfillment of communal desire or need is simple in its pragmatism but complex in its formal and aesthetic properties.

The fourth function is that of celebration. The context of celebration throughout plantation society, from South Carolina to Pernambuco, was the weekend dance assembly. Many people erroneously believe that the carnival in Trinidad was the most important period of collective celebration in the French Catholic islands. I do not believe that this is true at all. For most of the enslaved African populations, the most important context of celebration was the weekend dance assembly. This weekend dance assembly represented liberated time, time emancipated from the torturous and deadly routine of the plantation. It was at such assemblies that the enslaved peoples communicated desires and strategies of subversion and escape, and many rebellions were plotted at such assemblies. From as early as the seventeenth century right up until emancipation, the Antilles were circumscribed by laws which sought to control the dance assemblies. Some of these laws also involved the control or the banning of certain African drums as well as the banjo, the banjil, the banja, the shack-shacks, and so on. Thus, celebration could easily precipitate armed struggle, and this continued happening with the steel bands in Trinidad as late as the 1960s. Celebration and armed struggle were never too far apart in the steel band movement, and that circumstance too was a survival of the plantation mode which can easily be traced back to the old stick-fighting traditions where skill, dexterity, and aggressiveness were integral features of performance. In other words, performance itself was inseparable from competition, confrontation, facing the enemy, *sans humanité*, with stick in hand or with the rapier of the word or the sawn-off shotgun of the tenor steel drum. You can observe such references, for example, in David Rudder's calypso "Dust in Yuh Face" where he makes lyrical reference to "the tenor saw off," a representation of fierce steel band competition where panorama finals become like gun play, as though two gangs were facing each other at high noon. That is the image that Rudder is reworking in his calypso.

The fifth function of the music is that of social control, that is to say, through satire, mockery, *picong*, humor or, alternatively, through admonition, warning, moralizing, preachifying, prophesying, and doomsaying, the lyrics ridicule and damn whatever the particular calypso characterizes as socially unacceptable or unwarranted. Indeed, if you want to think of anything that has survived throughout the calypsos of the Antilles, it would be social commentary and control through the calypso's employment of these satiric or didactic modes of expression. We also find similar strategies in reggae and dub music as well. This function of social control, a function vital to the transmission of community values and social sanctions, is inalienably African as well. It is a way of drawing lines and saying that a certain type of behavior, either of the average clansman or of the ruler himself, has gone beyond socially permissible bounds.

Musicologists have frequently noted that in many African societies the singer, the storyteller, the griot, the poet, the man of words is privileged to criticize social foibles, though generally this criticism is made indirectly through a mask of words, imagery, proverbs, fables, and so on. Indeed, this question of masking is very important since it is one of the traditions which became transmitted through the various African and African-diaspora cultural practices mentioned earlier. The artistic strategy of masking is an important part of the calypso tradition and I think generally, too, of African traditions in the Caribbean. This African custom was maintained in the calypso and is alive today, as observed in those calypsos where politicians are anatomized with great frequency. Such dissection can be very fierce and has from time to time proven devastating. The calypsonian communicates with the people in a language that is simple, fairly direct even when the mask is employed, and in a manner that is very effective. Politicians these days work very hard to get as many calypsonians as they can on their side, and it is not unusual for calypsonians to sing on political platforms during elections. All platforms have some kind of singer and, indeed, in Trinidad there have been not only calypsonians but *chutney* singers, those predominantly Indo-Trinidadian singers who are exponents of the musical form known as *chutney*, a blend of Indian and African-diaspora musical forms. Sometimes, I suspect, if the songs rendered on political platforms are bad, the respective politicians might lose political office. Sometimes, calypsonians even sing on two or three political platforms, presumably to illustrate their impartiality, but I am not certain that impartiality is automatically implied when this is done, since many calypsonians are intensely partisan and sing to support their side.

In the middle of any government's political term, the calypsonians are likely to be critical because it is around this time that the population recognizes that promises will not be kept or cannot be kept, and the calypsonians begin to remind the government, in song, of their election promises and political manifestos. I am sure that the same thing occurs in Barbados with Barbadian calypsos as well as elsewhere in the Caribbean. I remember that when Barbadian calypsos came to be highly political, politicians didn't like them at all and tried in some way, either by threat or even by legal edict, to silence such calypsos. In fact, this effort at censorship has a long tradition in Trinidad. When the calypsonians are on the side of the politicians, generally there is no problem, but when there begins to be criticism, you get muffled hints that this kind of thing will not be tolerated. Nevertheless, the calypso, being flexible and having a long tradition of masking, can find various ways of evading censorship. Indeed, the stronger the tendency toward censorship becomes, the more clever the calypso becomes: for example, a singer like Bally would sing a calypso such as "Party Time," or David Rudder would sing "Madness," or Gypsy would sing "The Sinking Ship"—all during the same time period of the people's growing dissatisfaction with political affairs in Trinidad. On another occasion of dissatisfaction with governmental policies in Trinidad, Luta would sing "Good Driver" or Mighty Chalkdust would sing "Chauffeur Wanted," in which the driver of a bus, a thinly veiled reference to the governmental policies and practices at the time, was characterized as guilty of the reckless endangerment of passengers as well as pedestrians and others using the street. Thus we get examples of the calypsonian's use of satire and *picong* in the calypso, a type of artistic and critical form transplanted to the Caribbean and derived from earlier African-diaspora and African forms.

Let us move, then, to the sixth function, which is perhaps a minor function but which is still observable, and this is the function of praise, the commendation of outstanding achievement. There are a few calypsos which do this from time to time. When Trinidad won the World Netball Competition some years ago, for example, there were a few calypsos about that national success. When a national team wins, there is praise, but you do have some calypsos which are critical when a team happens to be losing. This is also a tendency of the praise song. The praise must be deserved and the praise is generally not uncritical praise. The scholastic achievements of former prime minister of Trinidad and Tobago, the late Eric Williams, were praised in calypsos, and his political charisma was often linked to his reputation for being a "great brain." All this was praised in song, but Williams also received his share of criticism through the calypso. Such praise-song practices have their African analogue. They represent the opposite of the satirical songs in that they celebrate the achievement of the hero, however the hero is defined, while satirical songs are the vehicles of the people's scorn when the hero proves to have feet of clay, as he or she usually does.

Other functions of the calypso also include the calypso as a sort of medium for news, gossip, scandal, that is to say, the calypso as popular newspaper narrating things which happen from day to day. This kind of calypso comments on interesting events taking place in the community or society. This function of the calypso continues today, although the narrative calypso is slightly on the wane. There are far fewer of them now than there were in the 1950s and 1960s, and one may justifiably say that the calypso provided the first narratives of the grass-roots people of these Caribbean islands. It is the calypso which identified the barrack-yard, for example, in the 1920s, even before the early Caribbean novelists started writing about the barrack-yard.[3] It was these early calypsos which told the society about what was happening in the bedroom, the domestic conflicts, the man-woman conflicts, the stereotypes in Caribbean gender relations, and so on. Indeed, if you want to know about these stereotypes, you can do nothing better than analyze the calypsos which focus on man-woman themes and you will get vivid, insightful details of all the stereotypes.

All of this is just by way of reestablishing my position that the calypso is a thing which, in all of its functions and in all of its shapes, is really a continuation of African musical traditions within a New World context. I also acknowledge that the calypso has reflected a constant and consistent interplay between its already multicultural African matrix and the various non-African cultures that the people of African descent encountered in the New World process of becoming Caribbean peoples. What I am positing is the idea of a culture-filled and culture-bearing African person who encountered, first of all, a variety of African cultures and practices on the New World plantation, and through a process of culture loss, assimilation, and syncretism within the polyglot African plantation community, designed a New World persona with which to encounter French Creole, Hispanic, English, Dutch, and a variety of other cultures including, afterward, Asiatic cultures as well.

This African/New World figure would undoubtedly borrow from the cultures of the dominant power structure, but the borrowing would take place against the background of a fairly powerful African matrix. Hence, French *patois*, or Creole French language, would reflect the Africanization of French, English Creole, the Africanization of the syntax of standard English, and so on. The rhythms of the Afro-Creole songs would be totally different from either English folk songs or French ballads, even when the stanza structures of the ballad began to be assimilated during the 1880s and the 1890s. Such assimilation of distinctly European features was not, as is sometimes claimed, a direct transmission from French troubadors, but was a direct result of social change taking place within the postemancipation society of Trinidad.

At the center of such social change was the beginning of substantial primary education in English during the 1870s and 1880s. Within two decades, a handful of bards emerged who were proficient in both Creole French and English, but chose to sing in the latter because English had emerged as the language of power and prestige. Here you observe the process of Caribbean identity taking shape, with a keen cognizance of the strategies and vicissitudes of power. Even the French Creole ruling elite had, by the 1870s, begun to send their own children to England, as well as Paris, to be educated, and in a number of instances they sent them to England rather than Paris. Thus, singing in English, the new bards mocked the more traditional *patois* singers and accused them of having no education and of being unable to master English prosody. They also adopted the grandiloquence of men of words and power in the society—the magistrates, the priests, the schoolmasters—all of whom would have been grand masters of the heavy rhetoric that one associates with the late nineteenth- and early twentieth-century English prose style. But even with respect to this grandiloquence, one can discern the transformation of the rhetoric of the educated class by the rhetoric of the semiliterate folk. Hence, there is signifying *robber-talk*, tea-meeting eloquence and a constant element of parody and word play, a mixture of emulation and mockery in the folk rhetoric which fed into the calypso after 1900. Again, these were features which were visible across the Caribbean.

Throughout the Caribbean, you have personalities who are champions of words and masters of rhetorical skills. In Guyana there was a man called Prophet Wills and in Trinidad there was someone called Gumbo Lai-Lai, very much the same kind of person. These rhetorical champions used words in fantastic ways and their rhetorical strategies found their way into the calypso. Thus by the end of this early period of the calypso's development, the function had begun to change. The *chantwell,* or lead singer, was no longer confined to whipping up the courage of the *battonier,* or stick fighter. In a context where the stick fighting had been officially prohibited in the 1884 Peace Preservation ordinance, the chantwell increasingly became a purveyor of strictly verbal challenges. In other words, in the old stick-fight tradition, the chantwell had to whip up the courage of his stick fighter, but after the period outlawing stick fighters, the contest became a verbal contest between singers. Hence you have the trading of insults, which used to be conducted in French Creole but now was happening in English. There were fierce battles of words which took place in the early twentieth century right up to the 1930s or so, when it became almost a vestigial part of the calypso tradition. There were personalities such as The Lord Executor, Senior Inventor, Richard the Lionheart, The Iron Duke, The Duke of Albany, The Duke of Marlborough. All of these were singers of that early period, and they were the kind of people who sang in what was then termed "the calypso war."

This gives us the background to the question of multiethnicity. The very form of the calypso reflects the multiethnicity of the Caribbean, and by just studying this one aspect of the calypso, one can learn a great deal about Caribbean identity through the lens of calypso. It is multiethnic and multicultural. At the present moment, the calypso is itself the product of influences and experimentation which speak of continuing transformation. If we consider the advent of *soca* in the calypso tradition, for example, we can observe a number of influences informing this development. There is Super Blue's "Soca-Baptist," where the Baptist chants, rhythms, hand clapping, and so on, become the basis of a calypso structure to which the Baptists in Trinidad took very strong objection. They felt that here was this calypsonian whose roots were Baptist and yet he was desecrating their religion. There is also *chutney* calypso—Indian music and the calypso mixed together—calypso music which focuses on Indo-Trinidadian themes and simulates certain forms of Indian music. There is also calypso-*parang,* where the Spanish Creole music traditionally associated with Christmas musical celebration in Trinidad is blended with calypso, as exemplified by Scrunter's "I Want a Piece of Pork." Again, the purists regarding the Spanish-derived music don't like this at all. They argue that this music which is traditionally in praise of the Anunciation and the Incarnation is now being made to serve secular purposes. But the process of change, which is actually an extension of the same multiethnicity and the confrontation and assimilation of different cultural forms, is continuing. In the 1930s and indeed as early as the opening of the twentieth century, there was the enormous impact of Latin American music on Trinidadian music. There was, for example, calypso-*rhumba*, Tobago-*kalinda*, and the *paseo* from Venezuela. Indeed, it is not too exaggerated a claim to suggest that part of Trinidad is Venezuelan, the southern part called Cedros. This area sometimes relates more closely to Venezuela than to the Trinidad capital, Port of Spain. So Venezuelan music, too, has had an impact on the Trinidad calypso.

I think these musical influences and the Caribbean reality of cross-cultural fertilization also tell us something about Caribbean identity. It often seems to be reaching out to something. It is outward looking as much as it is inward looking. We often talk about cultural imperialism, but I believe that many of these influences are received in the context of choice. I recognize that there is the market strategy of advertising and I know that there are external cultural impositions, but a lot of what is laid on us we accept—we choose, we want it. A number of calypsonians are highly focused on the internationalization of calypso, and this is a regional phenomenon. They seek to get calypso "out there," wherever that "out there" happens to be; and whether it is Japan or Scandinavia or Notting Hill carnival in England or the Toronto carnival in Canada, the calypsonians have a sense that there are norms and expectations associated with the internationalization of the calypso market. Thus, in order to satisfy some of these norms associated with the internationalization of the calypso, calypsonians do alter the form of their music. Chutney-soca, ragga-soca, soca-dub, even blends of Zouk, French Caribbean music, with soca have occurred; indeed any kind of blend that you can think of, the musicians have probably already experimented with it.

There is also a desire and necessity, some calypsonians say, to create music specifically for celebration purposes, for parties and dancing. Here the rule that function determines form also applies, in that if the function is to get a large number of people to jump at the same time, then you are likely to get songs which consist of the refrain "jump, jump, jump," and so on. There is constant repetiton. The music is absorbing the forms of advertising and participating in

self-advertisement. You create a slogan, a "hook line," and you repeat it. You look for an appealing melody and you repeat it. The
singers are trying to sell the product somewhere else, and it is interesting to observe how often this kind of song contains the line, "This
is soca music." There seems to be a need to identify the music for
markets outside the Caribbean region. So there is advertising tech-
nique influencing the form. There is also the question of involving
the listeners, the people who are celebrating the music, in the
music, so that you create lyrics which give them something to do.
There are many action songs in which the singer is telling the listeners, the party goers, what they should do. This may have started with
the Jamaican bandleader, Byron Lee, and his band, The Dragonaires.
I can remember as early as the 1960s in Jamaica that Lee's band created songs telling people to "put your hand in the air" and "Put
your foot and jump higher, higher, higher," and so on. Indeed,
Byron Lee has been attending Trinidad carnival for at least twenty
years. He popularized calypso music in Jamaica, and he moves between Jamaica and Trinidad.

In that form of music, the singer is in control. The singer has a
certain degree of power in the sense that she has the mike in front
of her. In addition, the lead singer and the band also demonstrate
increasing control over the medium as a result of the electronic nature of much of the music. A lot of the music has become what one
may call "mechanized joy." You are often listening to equipment
and the equipment gets larger and larger and the sound gets louder
and louder. Indeed, there is often a kind of inverse proportion between the quality of the music and its volume. You also have the
music taking a lyrical form where men suggest that they are in control of women. A lot of those lyrical commands consist of men telling
women what to do with different parts of their anatomy, and the
women often seem to comply. Since the late Lord Kitchener noted
some years ago that the "bum-bum" was the sugary part of the female anatomy, almost every calypsonian seems to have followed his
lead. There is hardly a calypso now without some reference to "bum-
bum." It is very repetitive, but it has become very popular.

Let us move now to the idea, or theme, of ethnic identity, which
is often juxtaposed to or set against national identity. Ethnic identity
often is represented as a more crucial identity formation than national identity. There are songs from the 1930s, for examle, addressing the connection between Caribbean identity and Ethiopia. There
were songs which interpreted World War II in racial terms. One calypso by Growling Tiger, for example, entitled "Let the White People Fight" speaks of the case of a veteran of World War II who re-

turns to the Caribbean, confined to a wheelchair; he also returns home with an English wife. Unable to find employment, he begins selling illegal "bush rum," but confined to the wheel chair, he is unable to escape the police when they seek him out for his illegal activity. They arrest him with the evidence and he is sent to jail where he eventually dies. While he is imprisoned and forgotten, the local white community cares for his English widow. Growling Tiger's calypso cites this scenario as a case to discourage any black person from enlisting in the white man's war. There were also songs which praised black achievement, songs about George Washington Carver and other such laudable persons of African descent. There was a great deal of black consciousness evident in several of the calypsos of this period. Thus, what you get in terms of Caribbean identity is the attempt to locate such identity in a wider context of pan-African consciousness.

In Trinidad you often get an oppositional tension between what is understood to be African-derived culture and what is understood to be Indian-derived culture. Many calypsos in Trinidad tend to address this tension, particularly the calypsos of someone such as Cro-Cro. He is a confrontationist and emphasizes black consciousness in many of his songs. An interesting situation around this issue of black consciousness in calypso was observed some years ago with the release of Black Stalin's "Caribbean Man." The actual title of the song is "Caribbean Unity," and the song was criticized by a number of sociologists and historians of Indian descent at the University of the West Indies campus, Trinidad. Their argument was that the song based its representation of Caribbean man and manhood on a type of Afrocentricity and thus did not mention Caribbean persons of Indian, Chinese, Syrian, Portuguese, or European descent. Basically, from an Afro-Caribbean perspective, there was little to fault about the song since it was telling black Caribbean men who had been stereotyped as irresponsible to be responsible toward their families and communities. It argued that the true basis for Caribbean unity would be cultural, but then defined Caribbean culture in terms of Afro-Caribbean icons. Many Indians in Trinidad objected bitterly to this and there was an enormous volume of correspondence in the local newspapers. Although the song did not in any way attack other racial or ethnic groups, there was a public outcry which suggested that because these other groups were not mentioned in the song, they were rendered invisible.

This episode told all Trinidadians, I think, a great deal about the idea of a national culture. If you are defining national culture in Trinidad, you have to have a definition that is flexible enough to cover various racial and ethnic groups, and no one has yet arrived at such a definition. Curiously, too, another Trinidadian calypsonian, Ras Shorty I, sang a calypso entitled "Om Shanti Oom," the chorus being based on a Hindu mantra. "Om Shanti Oom" was one of the most positive calypsos sung about the Indo-Trinidadian community. It was not proffering stereotypes, but was saying that there is much of value in Hindu culture and it further suggested that when anyone needed upliftment and deliverance from negativity, he or she could chant this mantra. The Hindu religious hierarchy objected to the calypso just as the Baptists had sometime earlier objected to Super Blue's "Soca Baptist." Thus, the problem posed is this: If you omit mentioning the Indo-Trinidadian community in these kinds of ca-lypsos, you are remiss in your omission. If, on the other hand, you do mention aspects of Indo-Trinidadian culture and practice in the calypso, even in a positive context as in Ras Shorty I's calypso, then you are still the likely subject of criticism. This gives us a glimpse of the problem of defining national identity in territories such as Trinidad, particularly if you are approaching things from a strong ethnic base. On the other hand, if you are not coming at identity from some ethnic base, the question becomes how clear and how valid is your definition of national identity? The problem, then, is to find some answer to the complexity of multiethnicity, some way of honestly and honorably representing all cultures on a common ground. It is going to take some time, and I don't think that Trinida-dian society is at present anywhere near solving this problem. The major debate about culture in Trinidad is going to be linked to these complexities of race and ethnicity for some time to come.

On a regional basis I think that these kinds of issues can only con-tinue to further complicate the question of regionalism. If you can-not solve the question of national identities and national cultures, it is difficult to see how you are going to solve the question of a re-gional identity. This difficulty has been, for a long time, one of the challenges of selecting the best cricketers from the region to repre-sent the West Indies cricket team. Each Caribbean nation has its in-terests in seeing a player from its shores selected for the regional team, and this can contribute to a host of complications. In Trini-dad, for example, this problem has frequently been evidenced in terms of there not being enough Indo-Trinidadian players on the West Indies team. It also sometimes expresses itself in terms of quite a number of Trinidadians of Indian descent supporting the players from the India or Pakistan teams in Test Matches against the West Indies.

There was a Test series in 1971, for example, in which West Indies captain Clive Lloyd declared the West Indies innings against India, giving India over 400 runs to make in order to win the match. During that home match, every single run the Indian team made was loudly applauded by Indo-Trinidadian cricket fans; whether it was a run because of a *leg-bye* or a *bye*, a push for a single, an edge, whatever it was, it was energetically applauded. After a while, you could see that this ironic support was having a troubling impact on the morale of the West Indies team as they must have wondered what was going on, since they were, after all, playing India on Caribbean home ground in Trinidad. This is clearly another example of the crucial and complex question of Caribbean identity illustrating the intricate and sometimes contradictory ways in which Caribbean peoples identify themselves. The calypso, with its ever-changing, dynamic form and its heterogeneous history, might not offer us a solution to the vexing question of Caribbean identity, but it surely offers us a viable medium by means of which we can approach such a complicated and profound concern.

Notes

1. Maureen Warner Lewis, *Guinea's Other Suns: The African Dynamic in Trinidad Culture* (Dover: Majority Press, 1991).

2. John Lovell, *Black Song: The Forge and the Flame. The Story of How the Afro-American Spiritual Was Hammered Out* (New York: Paragon House, 1972).

3. The "barrack-yard" refers to the overcrowded, roughly constructed dwellings which were part of an urban landscape of poverty and disenfranchisement in territories such as Trinidad during the colonial period.

The "Pleasures" of Exile in Selected West Indian Writing Since 1987

Evelyn O'Callaghan
University of the West Indies, Cave Hill, Barbados

> I followed a sea-swift to both sides of this text;
> her hyphen stitched its seams, like the interlocking
> basins of a globe in which one half fits the next
> into an equator, both shores neatly clicking
> into a globe . . .
> . . . .
> Her wing-beat carries these islands to Africa,
> she sewed the Atlantic's rift with a needle's line,
> the rift in the soul.
> —Derek Walcott, *Omeros,* chapter 63

I

SINCE the heady days when "West Indian Literature" as a term, and as a recognizable body of regional writing with its own specific characteristics, was being hailed as a valid field of academic study and an exciting new resource for indigenous readers; since the days when pioneering scholars like Kenneth Ramchand and Kamau Brathwaite and Cecil Grey created controversy in English departments at the University of the West Indies by insisting that local writers had as valuable a contribution to make as did "dead white males" like Milton and Wordsworth; since those days, a considerable volume of water has flowed under a number of bridges. For example, the very term is once more under interrogation. Thus, in 1994 Peter Hulme expressed the opinion that:

> "West Indian" is by no means as self-evident a term as it might at first appear . . . None of this is meant to suggest that "West Indian literature" is a meaningless concept; just that we need to pay some attention to the kind of category it is and to how it might differ from categories which seem at first sight analogous. So, to press matters a little further, we tend

to speak of "West Indian literature" rather than, on the one hand, a series of *national* literatures—Jamaican, Kittitian, Antiguan, and so on, and on the other hand the literature of a full geographical area— Caribbean or Antillean.[1]

Hulme's reflections are part of his effort to survey the criticism of *Wide Sargasso Sea* over the last twenty-five years in an attempt to "place" the novel. In the course of the article, he notes Ken Ramchand in 1980 pointing up the usefulness of teaching *Wide Sargasso Sea* as a means of raising the important questions, What makes a novel a West Indian novel? and What do we mean when we say that a writer is a West Indian writer?[2] Clearly, the term was—for some, anyway—no longer self-evident. Later, Hulme deals with other critical attempts to answer the question of what Rhys's novel might be: that is, "English or West Indian, colonial or postcolonial," modernist, feminist, or Third World? I have no intention of participating in what promises to be an ongoing debate, but merely want to use these questions to raise yet another set of issues concerning the literature in general, articulated by—among others—Susheila Nasta, in her *Wasafiri* editorial.

Aptly titled "The Scramble for New Literatures," Nasta's piece lauds the growing interest and proliferation of courses in "what are sometimes called the 'New Literatures in English' " at educational institutions in Europe and America. Noting the role of postmodernism in valorizing the shifting of boundaries—"where the disintegration is now celebrated at the center and where the margins have become the front line"[3]—she nonetheless has certain reservations about possibly overlooked "differences between the roots of the poetics of postmodernism and the realities of a movement in literature which derives originally from the realities of a history of colonialism. Whilst there has been a *fashionable* upsurge of interest among English departments in discourses of difference and otherness, there has also remained a disturbing tendency to continue to label, contain, and homogenize" ("E," 4). For some, the term West Indian literature is perhaps too all-embracing and needs to take account of national specificities; for others, the writing belongs within a much larger category: that of New Literatures in English or Post-colonial Literature. Nasta's problems with both these terms are perhaps relevant here: the former label tends "to cut the writing off from a history that often existed long before colonialism" and the latter to be too all-embracing for "areas making up almost two thirds of the world's geographical mass and with very different cultural and political backgrounds" ("E," 4).

Such concerns do not appear to bother Pico Iyer in the cover story of *Time Magazine* (8 February 1989). Reflecting on recent Booker Prize awards, Iyer notes the dominance of the current literary field in Britain by writers of non-British national and/or ethnic origin. "In 1981 the Booker went to Salman Rushdie's tumultuous, many-headed myth of modern India, *Midnight's Children*. In the eleven years since, it has been given to two Australians, a part Maori, a South African, a woman of Polish descent, a Nigerian, and an exile from Japan . . . There could hardly have been a more vivid illustration of how the Empire has struck back, as Britain's former colonies have begun to capture the very heart of English literature, while transforming the language with bright colors and strange cadences and foreign eyes."[4] The kind of writer Iyer has in mind is typified by Michael Ondaatje, a Sri Lankan of Indian, Dutch, and English ancestry, educated in Britain, long a resident in Canada, with siblings on four continents. The writing of such authors is unproblematically called World Fiction (the label includes Derek Walcott, Caryl Phillips, Jamaica Kincaid, and unspecified "Canadians writing of their native Barbados,"referring, I assume, to authors like Austin Clarke). The "centers of this new frontierless kind of writing are the growing capitals of multicultural life, such as London, Toronto and, to a lesser extent, New York" ("EWB," 46). Iyer recognizes that the phenomenon of the transformation of metropolitan literature and culture by immigrants is not new: "writers like V. S. Naipaul, Wole Soyinka and C. L. R. James have long staked distinguished claims beside the English writers they studied at school" ("EWB," 48). But he maintains that "the new transcultural writers are something different," and the rest of the piece illustrates why this is so.

My initial response to this division of much of West Indian writing into national subgroups or its assimilation into World Fiction or New Writing in English is one of undoubtedly chauvinistic unease. To illustrate: at a seminar sponsored by the British Council on "The Contemporary British Writer" (Cambridge, July 1990), I got into a rather strained discussion with an organizer as to whether one of the featured writers, Caryl Phillips, could be thus defined. Caryl himself put a nice end to the debate by asserting that he would be honored to be considered a West Indian author, to my immense satisfaction. But why bother about labels anyway? Partly, I think, because of the issue of power which certain labels either mask or confer. Introducing *Decolonising Fictions*, Diana Brydon and Helen Tiffin argue for the position taken by Max Dorsinville, whose "rejection of the synthesizing imperialism of the World Literature school in Comparative

Literature and . . . identification of new criteria for criticism based
on relations of domination"[5] they find persuasive. As they explain:

> Dorsinville concludes that we must re-formulate our questions, rejecting
> the distinction between national and international literatures to look in-
> stead at the distinction between dominated and dominating literatures,
> an undertaking that recognises the interconnections between literature,
> history and society and the primacy of relations of oppression for under-
> standing the conditions of literary and critical production. (*DF*, 24)

This "new criteria for criticism," a focus on power relations, is of
course central to postcolonial theory, and if we seek to discover a
blanket term under which to compare West Indian fiction with that
of other ex-colonial territories, postcolonial (even with all the concerns raised about this label) is to my mind more acceptable than
the others discussed above. This is, to a great extent, because the
concept of *difference* is central to postcolonial theory. Iyer acknowl-
edges that the "differences between the members of this group
[writers of World Fiction, also referred to as postcolonial writers]
are more striking than the similarities" ("EWB," 48) and that many
resent being lumped together. Indeed. And from a critical perspective, the editors of *De-Scribing Empire*, a study subtitled "Post-colonialism and Textuality," insist that we cannot adequately speak "of an
unspecified and undifferentiated post-colonialism."[6] Thus, while
the term is useful in setting up a certain context for comparing
widely differing texts, the texts themselves are not contained within
the term. Or, to put it another way, while I would consider all West
Indian writing to yield postcolonial readings, postcolonial texts are
not necessarily West Indian.

While the above ruminations on the contested nature of *West Indian* may appear tentative to the point of redundancy, I do think
these are important questions to raise. Crudely put, what Nasta is
implying in her editorial, what Hulme is acknowledging about Jean
Rhys, and what Iyer is—in part—publicizing, is that West Indian literature is a "hot property" in some circles today, and there are
many who are eager to stake a claim. Once more, the question of
power intrudes. Even among postcolonial critics, as Chris Tiffin and
Alan Lawson note in *De-Scribing Empire*, squabbles occur "precisely
because questions of language and speaking positions are often
really contentions over domains of ambiguous authority. The very
diversity of colonial experience with its Eurocentered hierarchies
has fathered a shadowy counterhierarchy in which he or she who
can most plausibly claim the kiss of the whip is accorded the preemi-

nent speaking position" (*DE*, 232). Such squabbles become even ludicrous, when so many of these critics "find themselves uncomfortably inside the residue of power structures they profess to oppose, and ambivalent beneficiaries of those structures" (*DE*, 232). But the notion of power engenders squabbles even among those who *accept* the term West Indian literature, as Hulme points out: "To be a 'West Indian novel' becomes . . . a privilege to be fought over in an argument that tells us more about different critics' notions of 'authenticity' than it does about the novel in question" ("P," 7).

However, let us leave the critics to their wrangling and turn now to some of the writers. In the rest of this essay, I focus on writers whose work demonstrates aspects of Iyer's transcultural definition. The products of colonial division and the internationalization of culture since the war, according to Iyer, they address an audience "as mixed up and eclectic and uprooted as themselves" ("EWB," 48). Mostly nonwhite, and choosing to write in English, both they and their writings derive from multiple homes, hence a concern with identity: "their central theme has been the plight of those who are torn between motherlands and mother tongues, the 'not quites,'as the Indian writer Bharati Mukherjee calls them. Most of all, they make a virtue of their hyphenated status. Instead of falling through the cracks, they hope, through their Janus-faced perspective, to straddle different worlds, and pick and choose from all traditions" ("EWB," 48). Could Iyer not be talking about the Caribbean writer? Certainly, there is a familiar ring to much of this for the student of West Indian literature. But the description is even more apt to a particular *subset* of West Indian authors, that "whole new generation of young black and Asian writers resident in Britain, whose vision is at once 'stereoscopic . . . plural and partial' [the unacknowledged quote is from Salman Rushdie in the Iyer article] and whose writing leaps the fences of a narrow literary nationalism" ("E," 4).

Specifically, I am referring to writing since 1987 by people (not necessarily young!) of West Indian origin who have been resident in Britain or the United States for much of their lives: V. S. Naipaul (specifically *The Enigma of Arrival*, 1987); Jamaica Kincaid (*Lucy*, 1990); and David Dabydeen (*The Intended*, 1991). I initially intended to include Caryl Phillips (*Cambridge*, 1991) and Derek Walcott (*Omeros*, 1990), but for reasons of space I will simply refer to these in passing.

The inclusion of Walcott's epic is somewhat anomalous, given that he has probably spent more of his life in the Caribbean than in the United States, where he is currently based, but he seems to me to evince what I call the transcultural imagination as much as any of

the other writers mentioned, if not more so. Like Phillips, Walcott
leads a peripatetic existence, dividing his time between the West Indies and "the metropole," and his poetry illustrates the *empowering*
nature of storytelling as a means of centering the coexistence of con-
tinuities and discontinuities, concordances and discordances. In
Omeros, we are presented not just with a transcultural but with a re/
versible (the pun is obvious) world. The poem fashions a network
that ranges between the city bases of the African and Asian diasporas
(London, Boston, New York, Toronto); England and its (former?)
colony, Ireland; the Mediterranean; the vanished world of the North
American Plains Sioux; Africa and the Caribbean. And all of these
connect in some way with the particulars of West Indian life—as
transcultural as you can get!

The point is not to establish the criterion of exile per se or to
bicker about how much time a writer spends in this place or that.
What I am trying to sketch is a vision shared by these texts, which
conveys a sense of what Lloyd Best has called "in betweenity." Most
of the writers mentioned above obviously have a quite different relationship with the mother country or metropole or imperial center
than did the West Indian authors who migrated to England or the
United States in the 1950s. Dabydeen's *The Intended* does not con-
jure up the world of Sam Selvon's *The Lonely Londoners;* Kincaid's
Lucy has little in common with Claude McKay's *Home to Harlem.* In
varying ways, the protagonists of the newer texts, as much as their
authors, are at home in the center; or, put another way, they are as
homeless there as in any other place. Indeed, in Beryl Gilroy's *Boy
Sandwich,* Vernella Fuller's *Going Back Home,* and Joan Riley's *The Unbelonging* one could argue that it is the *Caribbean* that is the imaginary
space. And as Mike Alleyne has proposed, certainly there is more
than a hint in Gilroy's text that a new generation of West Indians
have made their own space in Britain. What we have, then, is a body
of writing that evades labels, that is not exile-writing as much as it is
bicultural (or transcultural): as much at home in Britain or the
United States as in Guyana or St. Kitts or Antigua, and crucially informed by connections between the two worlds. Iyer situates the
writers "looking both ways at once, neither here nor there, [ending]
up citizens of nowhere, or somewhere in the mind" ("EWB," 48–
49). Or, I would add, somewhere in the text. Far from seeing this
in betweenity as a liability, Iyer maintains such writers *exult* in this
dividedness, in their liminal position. Again, Walcott springs to
mind. A self-proclaimed hybrid of Africa and Europe, a Protestant
in a Catholic island, an artist in a materialist society, his poetry and

drama have consistently explored with exuberance this interface of oppositions.

Perhaps this is a natural development of the "vision building" that Wilson Harris has long called for in West Indian literature, a limbo or gateway perspective that attends to antecedents, links and connections of all kinds in our much-divided postcolonial culture. Further, such a decentered vision can hope to transcend the stranglehold of binary oppositions inherent in the construction of a colonized people. As Tiffin and Lawson put it: "Post-colonial critics and theorists have found it difficult to postulate a way for the colonized to circumvent the cognitive patterns by which their world has been structured. The quest to defeat, escape or circumvent the pattern of binaries which has been identified as foundational to Western thought, for example, is seldom, if ever, attained" (*DE*, 6). Ah, but where the critics and theorists fear to tread, writers go boldly! Certainly, as I hope to demonstrate, the texts in question destabilize neat oppositional categorizing of the oppressor/oppressed, center/margin, black/white variety.[7]

In a postmodern world the whole question of identity has become much more problematic, and these texts offer a new twist (or twists) on a crucial theme in West Indian writing. Notions of insider/outsider, the central and the peripheral, are turned inside out. So, to quote Iyer again, these writers "make a virtue of their hyphenated status" ("EWB," 48); they both straddle a space between old and new homes, and inhabit two (or more) "half-homes" simultaneously. Obviously, with this kind of literature the notion of home—never unproblematic for the West Indian author—is rendered even more complex. In a sense, at-homeness has always evaded characters in, for example, the fiction of Naipaul and Rhys, and some twenty years ago, Kamau Brathwaite sounded the pervasive refrain in his *Arrivants*, "Where then is the nigger's home?" The literary responses suggested to the question ranged from Africa to Europe to South America and the Caribbean itself. Now, the newer writing answers, "nowhere and everywhere and above all, in between." A sense of homelessness in these texts is not necessarily enervating. Rather, the access to multiple cultures and language varieties and traditions can be seen as liberating, and the creative possibility for forging a new kind of Caribbean identity is, if difficult, at least an exciting alternative to a certain cynicism and often despair which pervaded the postindependence literature.

This is probably as good a place as any to elaborate on Best's phrase, "in betweenity." Delivering the annual Elsa Goveia Memorial Lecture at the Cave Hill campus of the University of the West

Indies (13 October 1994), Best referred to the Caribbean as the original global village. Populated by people from elsewhere, the West Indian colonies had their matrix in ambiguity. A majority of ex-Africans living within European institutions; a colony of exploitation wanting to be a colony of settlement; an open economy that was really closed; a fiercely democratic impulse coexisting with a rigidly authoritarian state, Best described the region as rooted in contradictions, schizophrenic in its political, economic, and social structures. The work of Harris in history, myth, and fable takes account of this stereoscopic orientation, as does Brathwaite's study of creolization, a process which—as Best emphasized—was different for different groups at different times. Given our plural and ethnically segmented societies, in which groups speak from *several* discursive positions, and the specifics of regional history, in betweenity and ambivalence form the essence of the West Indian condition. Further, the historical pattern of migration, interculturation, turbulence, and cleavages is repeated over and over, so that a further duality is apparent: the "great tradition" of induction/creolization and the "little tradition" of maintaining separate, residual group identity. And this, Best maintained, is the methodology of survival in the global village today throughout the world: simultaneous interfacing/creolization and maintenance of group cultural practices. West Indians *live* this betweenity and consider normal a condition that Best maintains is both dangerously unstable and potentially creative. In his view, what is necessary is a cosmology and historiography that takes account of this state, rather than defining the region continually as an adjunct of imperialism.

Taking up Best's emphasis on a pattern of cleavages, and relating this to the previously discussed question of homelessness, one can note in the focal texts an emphasis not so much on finding, leaving, or coming home, but on the process of *voyaging* between. I mean this in the widest sense: physical, spiritual, historical voyages and, of course, through writing, textual journeying. It does strike me that the selected texts rewrite/reverse as well as retrace the infamous middle passage, and in my analysis I try to attend to the ways the narratives play on/with the various points and patterns of the historical triangular trade which, in this context, I want to expand to include—a slight detour—North America. If my sketch of the transcultural vision is somewhat vague, the *political* ramifications of the texts are not, precisely because, as Tiffin and Lawson point out, "the boundaries of Empire are pervious at the level of discourse [and] text . . . These border-lands are the 'region where the control of representation can be contested' (Ashcroft 42). Boundary-drawing around colonial space(s), then, is less an exercise in taxonomy than a politics of representation" (*DE*, 234).[8] Redrawing the boundaries, therefore, can affect the whole politics of representation inherited from canonical English literature.

In the readings that follow, I attend to features of the transcultural imagination outlined above: the narrative perspective of what Rushdie calls "stereoscopic vision . . . in place of 'whole sight' "; a breaking down of apparently given binary oppositions; a problematizing of the old quest for identity theme; the blurring and/or bridging of borders and acceptance of a new kind of spatial homelessness that paradoxically makes for at-homeness anywhere; an attention to voyaging and the trope of the middle passage; and an insistence on the pleasures of in betweenity. Implicit in all these is the issue of language and literary tradition, which is most explicit in *The Intended,* but also informs the other texts: they no longer grapple with the oppressive weight of English and its influential if not hegemonic tradition, but confidently experiment with englishes *as well as* English.

II

It may be as well to begin with *The Enigma of Arrival*[9] for its apt title alone, but also because Naipaul has hardly been known as a writer whose work radically challenges boundary-drawing around colonial space. Indeed, Rob Nixon's study of Naipaul's work seeks to explain how his "almost programmatically negative representations of formerly colonized societies . . . make his readings of such societies easily assimilable to imperialist discursive traditions that run deep in Britain and the United States."[10] I would, however, like to suggest a reading of *Enigma* as a fine example of the "stereoscopic vision" outlined earlier. For one thing, the narrative situates itself—to the discomfort of many critics—firmly between the genres of autobiography and fiction. Generically, then, borders are deliberately blurred. Again, the work problematizes notions of subjectivity: we are presented with a narrating subject, the object of whose ruminations are largely himself. As Mark McWatt has shown, the narrator frequently adopts the tone of the older, wiser, and to some extent settled, subject, commenting on the inadequacies of the younger, colonial *arriviste*.[11] Above all, the text insists on a pattern of repetitive revision of perceptions and judgments so that certainties collapse and the only constant proves to be flux. This patterning is as much stylistic as it is thematic: the book is concerned with the journey of a colonial aspiring writer toward the realization of his profession, a voyage (both spatial and internal) that involves a process of profound revisioning and the ultimate acceptance of the "truth" that truth is relative, as is perception. The journey is never completed, no safe harbor is arrived at, and yet, paradoxically, some measure of reconciliation is possible with the acceptance of life's enigma. Acknowledging a "kinder, gentler Naipaul" in *Enigma* and *A Turn in the South,* Nixon suspiciously wonders at the fact that "this new self should first emerge from under its carapace when England and the United States shift from being merely his audiences to becoming the subjects of his prose. One observes an insidious correspondence between a change of heart and a change of location" (*LC,* 167). But Nixon has to acknowledge that *India: A Million Mutinies Now,* one of Naipaul's later works, and one that is firmly set in the Third World, also displays this quite different, optimistic approach from his generally splenetic attacks on non-Western societies.

David Streitfeld considers Naipaul's "true subjects" to be "the victims of the breakup of the colonial empires," but characteristically the writer is ambivalent about being labeled postcolonial: "One doesn't have to be a West Indian or Indian or English writer," says Naipaul, "just a writer." Yet, the condition of "exile" ("too pretty a word. One doesn't want to use it") is always present: "the feeling is always there."[12] Indeed. *Enigma* is consistently pervaded by this "feeling": "I . . . still felt myself to be in the other man's country, felt my strangeness, my solitude" (*E,* 13). Neither is there a home to return to: "my departure from my island in 1950—with all that it implied of homelessness and drift and longing—was final" (*E,* 152). Naipaul conforms wonderfully to Iyer's description of the typical writer of World Fiction: an Indian of West Indian descent, based in England, writing mostly about the Caribbean and, of late, Africa, Asia, the Middle East, and the United States, he evinces betweenity better than most. Yet the cultural coordinates of *Enigma* specifically locate the text as a kind of bridge between Britain and the West Indies. Certainly, it focuses on conditions of rootlessness, upheaval, cleavage, displacement, and marginality, but the narrator does find some kind of homecoming—as a writer—in the text, which revolves around links between the "idea of England" and an equally constructed "idea of the West Indies."

Part one of the text recollects the journey of the colonial to the mother country, but more importantly, the journey to *writing.* Its dominant metaphorical pattern is informed by vision and perception: what, after all, shapes the writer and what the writer shapes. The first two pages alone reiterate images of sight, clear and partial: "I could hardly see . . . I saw . . . I saw what I saw very clearly. But I didn't know what I was looking at" (*E*, 11–12). For the colonial, a long history of imposed visions shape his perception, visions learned from a "third-standard reader [f]ar away in my tropical island, before I was ten" (*E*, 12) and circulated in canonical European texts. For the *writer*, therefore, when he reports that "I saw with the literary eye, or with the aid of literature" (*E*, 22), it is through English literature and art that his vision is mediated. Hence, intertextuality and literary allusions proliferate: hay in a shed "made me think of the story about spinning straw into gold and of references in books with European settings to men sleeping on straw in barns" (*E*, 17); the sight of Jack's father is "Wordsworthian, the subject of a poem Wordsworth might have called 'The Fuel-Gatherer' " (*E*, 26). Similarly, the narrator's understanding of what kind of creature a writer might be is also very much constrained by that tradition. So that Trinidad and family and the past "did not seem to me suitable to the work, which was about a more epic vision of the world" (*E*, 100); the "idea of a literary life [is, of necessity] in another country" (*E*, 108).

Yet the past and Trinidad intrude into the writing of this text. Cows on an English hillside recollect "the cows in the drawing on the label of the condensed-milk tins I knew in Trinidad as a child," fantasy cows that were nothing like the island cattle, just as these English cows are no "lowing herd winding o'er the lea here, as in Gray's 'Elegy' " (*E*, 80). Gray's "Elegy" and cows on a condensed-milk tin in Trinidad, English cows and Trini cattle: a bovine instance of the stereoscopic vision bridging two worlds. This double-vision recurs in the writing. So the "shape and texture of this snow drift reminded me of . . . a Trinidad beach" (*E*, 45), the old world of England overlaid with images from the New World, the present landscape seen through the filter of the topography of the West Indian past. Helen Tiffin argues that this attention to the presence of the Caribbean in a celebration of the English countryside serves to defamiliarize England, to show its constructed nature, as later in Naipaul's novel "there is simultaneously a recognition of the imperial construction of Trinidad, and the retracing, through the text, of that fault line to the English countryside with the invisible landlord of the estate still relentlessly spinning his textual webs from the imperium."[13]

The landlord's book, with its "joke knowledge" of Africa (*E*, 253) is paralleled with the young colonial writer's joke knowledge of England, or more properly with the idea of England learned as part of his colonial education, which proves responsible for his faulty vision, for "seeing what I wanted to see" (*E*, 27). Further, the gaps between what "garden," "house," "estate" and "landlord" *mean* in an English, as opposed to a Trinidadian, context, lead the narrator to an awareness of the "cultural grounding of English texts and their language" ("RR," 41). So that the stereoscopic vision, operating through these several doublings, leads to recognition of the fact that meaning is not universal, that the truths of English literature are not universally true, and a vision that sees only through this literature is partial and faulty. Thus, *Enigma* moves away from an articulation of marginality to a sense of assured centeredness by stripping away the self-deceptions, fantasies, and prescripted joke knowledge of the colonial writer and his idea of England.

Indeed, the narrator comes to see, as it were, archeologically, that is, with the realization that what is seen consists of layer upon layer of imposed visions. "Shepard and Constable—they had imposed their vision on an old landscape. But on their vision was imposed something else now" (*E*, 170). And in a sense, what is imposed in this text is the stereoscopic vision of the postcolonial writer, one which effects what Tiffin calls "the 'othering' of England" ("RR," 38). As a child, the narrator admits to projecting everything he read (Dickens, for example) on to the streets of Port of Spain (*E*, 155). As an adult writer, he reads his English landlord by "projecting myself on him" (*E*, 254). Both instances can be interpreted as the kind of appropriation—in reverse—practiced by the imperial conqueror. In addition, the voyage to the mother country involves an awareness of its fictionality: the glory is gone, its antiquity is an illusion, its permanence a facade as artificial as its restored churches and farmhouses (*E*, 49). Permanence is built on ruins, only to become in turn a ruined site for future building; the writer sees the strata simultaneously and learns what recurs as a motif of this narrative: "Change was constant. People died; people grew old; people changed houses; houses came up for sale. That was one kind of change. My own presence in the valley, in the cottage of the manor, was an aspect of another kind of change" (*E*, 34). As the New World man imposes his presence on the English countryside, buying his land and staking his claim, so newly marginalized citizens of the mother country drift, homeless and rootless, through the valley; the new dispossessed invade the estate (*E*, 270, 274).

This ironic juxtaposing and reversing (a kind of translating of what was found on arrival) is matched by the crablike movement of the novel, which consists of a constant process of revising. McWatt describes this as a kind of "infinite rehearsal." Perception is revealed as misperception, followed by adjustment of perception, only to be revealed as further misperception, and so on ad infinitum. The narrator's realization that his expectations about Leslie's looks (*E*, 66), or his discovery that the man taken to be a farmer is in fact only the farm manager (*E*, 26), demonstrate that acquiring knowledge is, in *Enigma*, "also a process of divesting [oneself] of a number of pre-judgements and false impressions" ("WIWS," 21). Hence, the reportage is undermined from the start by qualifiers. Terms and phrases such as "I had imagined," "it seemed to me," "there appeared to be," "falsely suggested," "apparently," "possibly," "romance," "fantasy," proliferate and clog the narrative, signaling the illusory nature of observation.

Naipaul (rather like Rhys) is fond of the parenthetical disclaimer, which virtually invalidates what is said at the moment of the saying. Jack's garden "suggested to me (falsely, as I got to know soon enough) the remnant of an old peasantry" (*E*, 22); "the old river bed (as I thought), sloped up" (*E*, 15); perception and its revision are contained in the same semantic moment. Rather like Harris, Naipaul's narrator is given to an "x or y" patterning: "the owner or the builder of the house," "shaped like a hut or cottage" (*E*, 17). The effect is of not-quite equivalences, highlighting the potentially false nature of appearances and judgments, the *related* nature of differences. Intertextual links, including references to Naipaul's own body of work; the co-presence of temporal or geographical spaces; the presence of the narrator not just as subject and object of the story but as marginal to, and agent of, change (*E*, 52); journeys that intersect and overlap (*E*, 136); journeys that parallel physical and internal voyages; all these devices I cite as evidence of stereoscopic vision.

One final illustration. In part two of *Enigma,* a complex of related stories is sketched. The story of Jack's garden is revealed to be an alternative version of the story read into the Chirico painting (the title of which is shared by this particular novel), which in turn is a version of the "Africa book" he was writing, which triggers the memory of another manuscript whose themes are, in a sense, those of West Indian history. And woven into the network is a semi-autobiographical account of Naipaul/the narrator's career, which holds the web together (*E*, 91–96). Structured by voyages of all kinds between old world and new, center and periphery, past and present, *The Enigma of Arrival* seems to me to be part of a new departure in West Indian fiction, a new development out of preexisting trends. Bicultural in setting, concerns, and narrative strategy, it embraces homelessness as the precondition of an acceptance of home, one which is sensitively aware of the constructed nature of both subjectivity and place, and yet is guardedly positive. "We had made ourselves anew"

(*E*, 317); "we remade the world for ourselves" (*E*, 318): as a statement of West Indian identity, this is both a truism and a revelation. For what Naipaul's narrator-persona has done is to "make" himself and his community *in the text*, out of alienation, rootlessness, cleavage, and betweenity. As Kincaid does in *Lucy*, he posits that this recreation—one which transcends the traps of historical containment in binary oppositionality (or alterity)—results from a new way of seeing, an alternative vision that insistently relativizes and stresses the partiality of judgment, so that the transcultural imagination, epitomized in Walcott's *Omeros*, but present in all the texts I have mentioned, is both the most reliable bridge between us all and illustrative of a more sustainable subjectivity.

III

Jamaica Kincaid's *Lucy* is, like *Enigma*, set outside the West Indies, this time in the United States. As in Naipaul's novel, the alien environment is already known. And, as in *Enigma*, knowledge turns out to be false. The long-desired famous buildings, important streets, spectacular bridges, appear "ordinary, dirty, worn down from so many people entering and leaving them in real life," forcing the recognition that they had been for the narrator "fixture[s] of fantasy."[14] And soon after arrival, Lucy begins to overlay this new world with the sights, sounds, and smells of her West Indian island home. This is not simple immigrant nostalgia, for Lucy has a profoundly ambivalent relationship with her motherland and arrives having "long ago . . . decided not to miss anything" (*L*, 82). As in Naipaul's text, the opening pages of Kincaid's narrative are dominated by images of imperfect vision: it is night, and despite "lights everywhere . . . I could not see anything clearly" (*L*, 3). Aware that the reliability of her old perceptual patterning is in question—the sun shines, but there is no warmth; the normal links of cause and effect are in abeyance—Lucy observes her new home through the filter of the cultural values of the old. The old home, however, being the New World, has traditionally been constructed—even by the narrator herself—in terms borrowed from the old, from Europe. Inevitably, the result of this multiple vision is to implicitly compare and judge, and America usually comes off worse. Mariah, Lucy's employer, is seen to be beautiful; but it is a pallid beauty, untested by pain or passion, and the narrator prefers the scarred, blemished face of Sylvie from home, a friend of Lucy's mother who had been bitten by another woman in a fight over a man. This "embrace of hatred" for the sake of passion is something Lucy feels sure she too will bear (*L*, 25). Similarly, recollection of "the big blue sea I was used to" asserts itself when a famous lake—again, already known to the narrator from "books"—disappoints on first view: "it looked so ordinary, gray, dirty, unfriendly, not a body of water to make up a song about" (*L*, 35).

Her stereoscopic gaze is particularly sensitive to the hypocrisy, masking, and deceit necessary for the projection of the facade of the perfect happy family, with whom Lucy comes to live as a nanny. Behind the farce, she soon sees, is a disintegrating marriage. Patricia Harkins has argued that Lucy is well-trained in seeing beyond appearances, given her own "long history of masking the truth, a skill her mother taught her."[15] This skill is also the result of her colonial upbringing and education into imitation of things English: as Lucy admits, at Queen Victoria Girl's School at the age of ten, "I was then at the height of my two-facedness . . . outside, I seemed one way, inside I was another; outside false, inside true" (*L*, 18). But notions of true and false, appearance and reality, are in fact not as simple. For the narrator's consciousness, conditioned by an alternative epistemological framework in the West Indies, admits of no such clear binary opposition: "I came from a place where there was no such thing as a 'real' thing, because often what seemed to be one thing turned out to be altogether different" (*L*, 54). Kincaid has elaborated on this distrust of reality in one of her many interviews,[16] clearly linking it with the normal acceptance in Antigua of the paranormal (obeah, spirit possession, the appearance of the dead to the living).

To this, we might add Kincaid's dismissal of the realist tradition in writing: as she opines in the same interview, the notion of representing in a story anything "as it is, is patently absurd." Whatever the source, the textual motif of the deceptive nature of appearances—aptly contained within a prose that on first reading is strikingly lucid and apparently simple—has the dual effect of relativizing cultural practices and transcending binary oppositions inherent in Western metaphysics that tend to hierarchize those cultural practices. So whether, as Karen King-Aribasala maintains, "Lucy's voyage of discovery then is involved in unmasking the deceit of the West"[17] or revealing her *own* self-deceit, the novel has the effect of putting in question easy truths of all kinds. Nothing is what it seems, differences are relatively similar and similarities different. Weeds at home are treasured houseplants in the United States (*L*, 99); Mariah's best friend is also the cause of her misery; "days go by too slowly and too quickly" (*L*, 140); the mistress is revealed to be far less resourceful than the maid; and so on. The point is that *Lucy*'s simple narrative insists, as much as Naipaul's labyrinthine one, on the relativity of truth and the constructedness of perception.

Lucy is also similar to *Enigma* (and indeed to the other texts discussed below) in its focus on voyaging. The story concerns a young West Indian girl's arrival in the metropole and her clearing of a space there where she can discover and make a life. But in many ways, she never truly leaves the past life/place that is carried within. She never really *arrives;* if the text begins with an arrival, it ends with a departure, as Lucy finally embarks on her new life as a writer. The text itself, then, is a voyage, a (w)rite of passage. And as Alison Donnell suggests, given Lucy's arrival in a fallen, wintry world, with the promised land falling far short of her dream, neither her exile nor arrival are complete.[18] Far from arriving at a destination she can live in/with, the narrative is a record of a restless, ongoing journey in quest of "accommodation" (as used by Naipaul in *A House for Mr. Biswas*).

Continuing to play on the theme of the voyage, most readers have noted the text's troping on the middle passage. Lucy's awareness of the place in which she has been put, her station as it were, calls up not only the "maid's room" but also the hold of a slave ship. Her room is "like a box—a box in which cargo traveling a long way should be shipped" (*L,* 7). Yet, even as the narrative thus places her within a fixed set of textual and social relations determined by the discourse of slavery and imperialism, it is undermined. "But," the passage continues, "I was not cargo." Within the inherited discursive pattern that operates in this America, if Lucy is not "cargo," the transplanted slave, then what is she? Again the text subverts expectations. For the voyage motif is used to draw strikingly inverted parallels with Columbus's journey to the New World. King-Aribasala makes a cogent case for reading *Lucy* as a rewriting of Columbus's voyage of discovery and conquest. Furious that "the origin of my presence on the island—my ancestral history—was the result of a foul deed" (*L,* 135), Lucy takes swift revenge. As King-Aribasala puts it, "she becomes the deceptor par excellence for a time, the Lucifer or devil who will 'deplete the moral resources' of white America to her own advantage" ("CC," 4). In other words, Lucy imitates Columbus, arriving only in order to rename, conquer, and exploit. The moral corruption of Paradise, a Paradise lost forever with the advent of men from the Old World, will be repatriated in the guise of a woman from the New World, who has learned the colonizer's methods very well indeed.

However, King-Aribisala posits that the project does not, in effect,

follow the original plan. For Lucy sickens with disgust at the perpe-
tration of a cycle inherently poisoned by colonial discourse, "a scene
of conquered and conquests" (*L*, 30), within which she too is interpellated even as she tries to *reverse* its terms: "a scene of brutes
masquerading as angels and angels portrayed as brutes" (*L*, 30). In
effect, she changes the terms of the engagement. Built into the foundations of imperialist discourse is the binary opposition of conqueror and conquered; oppressor and oppressed; subject and object; master and slave. But the thrust of Kincaid's narrative is away
from such neat, Manichean categorization. Further, Lucy quite explicitly refuses to be interpellated as "cargo," but neither is she willing for long to embrace the role of conqueror.

Therefore, having made a number of conquests (mainly, but not
exclusively, sexual) and exploited both place and people in a number of ways, Lucy comes to see that cultural contact is not necessarily
synonymous with corruption, is not necessarily to be played by the
master's poisoned rules. After all, what Columbus discovered in the
West Indies was largely an illusion, and much that came after was
founded on economic and religious doctrines which also *determined*
reality. So Lucy opts out of that way of seeing, which, in any case, the
narrative (like that of *Enigma*) has been subtly undermining all
along by insisting on the relativity of perception, judgment, and
value. Even as the narrative seems to gear itself up for righteous
anger at Columbus and his heirs, it deflates the prescribed response.
For example, Columbus is held in contempt for naming Lucy's island only in passing (*L*, 135). But just before this passage is an account of Lucy's deep shame that "someone who was born on the
other side of the world from me but had visited this island on which
my family had lived for generations" knows and names her island
intimately while Lucy "had never set foot on three-quarters of it"
(*L*, 134). Who, here, has the right to name? Again, the Columbus
reference is followed by Lucy's proud declaration of her anticolonial
stance. Then the defiant rhetoric gives way to enumeration of the
rather petty reasons for her dislike of "the descendants of the Bri-
tons": "for being unbeautiful, for not cooking food well, for wearing
ugly clothes, for not liking to really dance, and for not liking real
music. If only we had been ruled by the French: they were prettier,
much happier in appearance, so much more the kind of people I
would have enjoyed being around" (*L*, 136). Such accusations shift
the tone of the passage yet again, toward an aesthetic order, and
reader response is once more destabilized. Is this serious postcolonial politics or superficial essentialist stereotyping? The narrative
consistently shifts gear, throws up paradoxes, fosters and explodes

illusions, blurs boundaries between binarisms, and in doing so suggests that there are always other types of envisioning than those historically imposed.

Perhaps the most consistent feature of Kincaid's protagonist Lucy (apart from her unhappiness) is her refusal of prescribed subject positions. In her sexual relationships, her main concern is to evade ownership: "the moment he got the idea he possessed me in a certain way . . . was the moment I grew tired of him" (L, 155). She refuses to be a nurse, the career mapped out for her; she refuses all that was "expected" of her by her mother and "polite" society: "a sense of duty to my parents; obedience to the law and worship of convention" (L, 133). She rejects being placed, whether in terms of nationality—"from the islands"—or in terms of gender: " 'Woman? Very simple . . . she is a womb, an ovary; she is a female—this word is sufficient to define her' . . . My life was at once something more simple and more complicated than that" (L, 132). Lucy identifies with Gauguin, understands "finding the place you are born in an unbearable prison and wanting something completely different" (L, 95), a place "where no one knew much about me; almost no one knew even my name, and I was free more or less to come and go as pleased me" (L, 158). Such freedom, unplaced, unknown, unbelonging, is necessary for the continual self-construction which preoccupies Lucy: "I understood well that I was inventing myself" (L, 134).

This quite self-conscious problematizing of the whole notion of identity is something Kincaid has herself spoken about many times. In an interview with Gerhard Dilger she refuses the linking of black people to "traditional things," and denies any "African traditions" in her own work.[19] Similarly, she finds obsession with racial classification absurd ("I," 23), as is any fixed distinction between "the people's language" and "the imperial language" ("I," 22). For Kincaid, like Naipaul, contradiction and flux *is* the ground of life and the source of creativity. Quite explicitly, then, she refuses to be fixed: "In this world I live in, I'm nobody, and it's quite fine with me. I choose that. I'm not African, I'm not anything" ("I," 24). One could argue that the distaste for being categorized informs the creation of "Jamaica Kincaid." For the writer has given so many interviews on this subject, that it has become a story of its own. It goes something like this: Elaine Potter Richardson grew up (unhappily) in colonial Antigua. Always aware of being different, she migrated at sixteen to the United States in order to "make sense of myself to myself" ("I," 21). After various career switches and transformations of appearance, she became "Jamaica Kincaid," who eventually became a respected writer, who gave interviews in which she told and retold the story of that becoming.

"I . . . invented a self that I wanted to be, which was a dissenting person," she tells Pamela Muirhead: "I just sort of was always in the process of making myself up." So far, so good. But Kincaid has also repeatedly stated that "practically everything I've written is autobiographical."[20] And certainly there are clear parallels between events in the fictional works and those in the story of Jamaica Kincaid. Thus, readers delve into the fiction for glimpses of the real life. But *whose* real life? That of "Jamaica Kincaid"? But that too is a fictional identity, and a carefully constructed one. Thus, the writer creates and recreates a public persona in order to evade ownership, in order to put a layer between the self in the texts and, as George Lamming puts it, "the you that's hidden somewhere in the castle of your skin." Apart from the amusing connotations of this—for example, the writer reading the thesis of an earnest undergraduate who has found Jamaica Kincaid in, say *Lucy*, when Jamaica Kincaid is a persona constructed precisely for the media/journal interview pages—my point is that the indeterminate nature of identity is clearly an important preoccupation for writer and text.

In the end, *Lucy* can be read as an achievement of identity, but of a particularly *textual* kind. In the sense that the narrative begins with a nameless I enumerating the various persons she has been—"your past," thinks Lucy, is simply "a collection of people you used to be and things you used to do" (*L*, 137)—and ends with the narrator naming herself, to this extent the novel shows Lucy writing herself into a subject. But as this naming is done in the notebook given her by Mariah, a book within the novel, the identity exists as a construction of, and solely within, the text. "On the surface, something natural, something taken for granted, and yet underneath one could find worlds" (*L*, 159): always aware of the subtext behind the surface, the sensibility is always that of the artist. Hence, Lucy first tries photographic representation/transformation of her world, and finally turns to writing, fully aware that what's highlighted or foregrounded always changes the meaning of the picture. Like *Enigma*'s narrator, Lucy comes to see her hyphenated status, her situation between two worlds, her betweenity, as an asset. In fact, it is an essential attribute in the sophisticated perception of the complex interactions of the powerful and the powerless, a theme that predominates in the novel, and informs Lucy's history, Kincaid's fiction, and, indeed, any concept of West Indian identity.

IV

The final text examined in depth here is David Dabydeen's *The Intended*, which illustrates McWatt's assertion that "the West Indian who grew up and was educated in the colonial system lived in two different worlds."[21] These consisted of the Creole-speaking world of home and the village, and the world of school and English literature and history and Standard English: a doubleness portrayed in George Lamming's *In the Castle of My Skin* and Merle Hodge's *Crick Crack Monkey* and Olive Senior's two collections of stories. Hence, McWatt posits that "the seeds of trans-culturalism were already present in the experience of growing up West Indian. West Indians have always inhabited more than one culture, given the history and development of the region. Within West Indian societies, however, the would-be writer lived too close to the polarized and mutually hostile factions that Lamming describes. He/she needed distance in order to escape their claims upon his/her person and allegiance and also in order to gain perspective" ("L," 2). *The Intended* charts the education of such a writer-in-exile, illustrating Best's paradigm of between-ity in the structuring tension between the pull to assimilate, integrate into the new, and the desire to retain some of the different cultural markers of the old home.

Even as the narrator names his *intended* course in life: "I . . . longed to be white, to be calm, to write with grace and clarity"[22]—to be, in short, an English writer—the intrusion of his recollected Guyanese childhood and its Creole-speaking voices demonstrate the insistence of a former identity asserting itself. Similarly, the text contrasts the narrator's desire for Englishness and that of (another immigrant) Joseph's resistance of assimilation. Further, the narrative itself works to subvert the narrator's intention in spite of himself. So McWatt points out that the very features of Englishness the narrator chooses to embody his desire—"the craftsmanship of English china, coaches, period furniture, harpsichords, wigs, English anything" (*I*, 197)[23]—serves to trivialize and make irrelevant the intention by reducing it to an arbitrary list of *things*. The constant eruption of Creole voices into the text refuses the silencing that the narrator wants to impose on his denigrated home culture. Like *Lucy*, the destabilization of the old center/margin binary pair is implicit in a novel that unsparingly describes the rottenness which marginal man sees at the heart of the imperial center:

> where people cared nothing for family, dumping their parents in old people's homes, marrying and breeding and divorcing and bequeathing

the children to the welfare, abusing their own kids or abducting other peoples'; where every Sunday saw the churches empty and the pubs packed with dart-throwing louts relaxing from the hooliganism of the football match the day before, building up their strength for next Saturday's warfare. (*I*, 21)

Indeed, it is in far-off Guyana, in the map of lines on his grandmother's cracked feet that "all the pathways of the world" (*I*, 37) converge and are centered. Despite the setting of the novel, life in the metropole, this work shares with those previously discussed a privileging of the migrant's perspective over that of the metropolitan native.

Like *Enigma* and *Lucy*, *The Intended* deliberately blurs the generic distinction between autobiography and fiction: events in the author's life are paralleled in that of the young narrator. And as a corollary, one of its central concerns is the exploration of the narrator's subjectivity. Here, too, this identity is a hyphenated one. A West Indian in England, the narrator is both insider and outsider. He identifies with the exile's condition, but is frequently made aware of his differences from black West Indians:

> I come from their place, I'm dark-skinned like them, but I'm different, and I hope the whites can see that and separate me from that lot. I'm an Indian really, deep down I'm decent and quietly spoken and hard-working and I respect good manners, books, art, philosophy. I'm like the whites, we both have civilisation. (*I*, 177–78)

But of course, the Asian diaspora is no more homogeneous than the black. The differences between Shaz, Patel, Nasim, and the narrator are far greater than their similarities so that "the only real hint of our shared Asian-ness was the brownness of our skins. Even that was not uniform" (*I*, 5). A stereoscopic awareness of simultaneous links and differences dominate his consciousness. He is not black West Indian, but the black West Indian Joseph is "my dark self" (*I*, 196). As an Indo-West Indian, he perceives his difference from "real Indians," but knows that "these people were yet my kin" (*I*, 15). And as an educated person, one who can speak the language and "decipher the texts," he is "no longer an immigrant" (*I*, 195) but rather an insider for whom "all the people I knew as a child in another country were fading . . . were like the characters in my geography textbook, vividly illustrated but unreal all the same" (*I*, 27). Yet the text underscores the fact that neither is he English: "I can't live like white people" (*I*, 202). Even the memory of Guyana, with its poverty, mud, and many drunken aimless lives, both claims and repulses

him. Faced with this compound/nonidentity, the course of action
chosen is that taken by Lucy and the narrator of *Enigma:* to claim
unbelonging, the undefined and uncategorizable identity of the
permanently detached outsider, connected with but ultimately peripheral to all claims of race, nation, and culture. In a sense, like
Stephen Dedalus, this is to choose the role of the writer, who creates
his/her subjectivity out of, and only in, the text.

Along with the other works analyzed here, *The Intended* sees the
new world of England (that is, the Old World) through the filter of
the old home, the New World. The Caribbean is continually inscribed on England. With no transition, a walk down Bedford Hill
(in "old Albion") becomes a remembered walk with his grandmother from the bus stop at Albion village in Guyana (*I*, 28); a ride
on the London Underground recalls a bus trip on the "Duke of
Kent" in Berbice (*I*, 18); memory fabricates what is seen, so that the
narrator wonders whether his English life is really a dream he is still
having, while dozing in his grandparents' hammock (*I*, 30). The
imaginative world-bridging effected by this narrative patterning also
fractures the program of assimilation that the narrator so assidu-
ously pursues. Further, it defamiliarizes ways of seeing, and prepares
the reader for the radically different epistemological framework that
Joseph epitomizes.

Crazy he may sound, but in the context of the text's rapid to-and-
fro between worlds Joseph makes a lot more sense than initially appears to be the case. With impeccable postmodernist logic, Joseph
points out the relativity of representation: "A film is like a mirror . . .
everybody who watch it see something different" (*I*, 157). Elsewhere, he notes the inherent hierarchization of perceptual fields.
Illiterate and technically inept, Joseph is streets ahead of the educated narrator when it comes to imaginative insight: "I can't read
nor write but I can see" (*I*, 107). The narrator, by contrast, *can* read
and write, can interpret the texts of power, but as the novel self-
consciously demonstrates, his sight (like that of Lucy and the narrator of *Enigma*) is clouded by fantasy, what he expects or wants to see.

I have not dealt with the pervasive topic of sexuality in *The Intended*, but it is here that such blindness is most obviously exposed.
A white girlfriend is not simply a woman, but a symbol of already
prescripted desire:

> "But you are fragrant, you are everything I intended," I blurted out, the
> words seeming to come from nowhere, and as soon as they were uttered,
> sounding foolish. In one accidental sentence I had finally confessed all
> the dreams I had stuttered out to her in a year of meetings, always trying

to structure the expression of my desire for her so as to make it imper-
sonal, philosophic, universal, but always failing, my plain needs leaking
through the cracks in words. (*I*, 243)

Of course, this is disingenuous. The novel has painstakingly set up
an intertextual parallel with Conrad's *Heart of Darkness* in which
Kurtz's intended functions as a metonym for all the illusions about
civilization he must face, when confronted with the brute reality of
Africa. Here the white girl serves a similar purpose: she represents
to the narrator the idea of England to which he wants so much to
belong, even as he is increasingly aware that it is a constructed fantasy. The point is, however, that it is not the educated narrator who
can access what leaks "through the cracks in words," but the illiterate, paranoid Joseph. Mocking the narrator's "readerly" interpretations of English literature, safe meanings conforming to a strict set
of received rules ("a mechanical trick," *I*, 163), Joseph—his "dark
self"—opens a new space in the text with his "writerly" intuition of
what literature is all about. As the narrator pontificates on pentame-
ter and trochee in poetry, Joseph interrupts:

> "Poetry is like bird," he said, "and it gliding or lifting and plunging,
> wings outspread or beating and curving, and the whole music is in the
> birdwing."
> "Birdshit!" Shaz retorted on my behalf, convinced of my superior
> book knowledge of Form.
> Joseph was equally adamant. "What you doing with your pentating
> and strokee and all dem rules is putting iron-bar one by one in a spa-
> cious room so the bird . . . breaking beak and wing against the wall trying
> to reach the sunlight." (*I*, 95)

Somewhat strained, perhaps, the analogy highlights the limitations
of "superior book knowledge of Form," ironically of course, given
the very obviously structured nature of the text in which this observation occurs! But what is being questioned here is more than traditional methods of Lit. Crit. *Knowledge*, per se, is being held up for
inspection. For the novel constantly valorizes "erudition," "knowledge," "true talent" from the start. The trouble is, these terms apply
variously to knowledge about sex, erudition as to rock music lyrics
or film lore, talent for picking pockets as well as to "book knowledge." Thus, the narrator's "brightness" (academic ability), which
is invested with so much prestige as an avenue to power, to Englishness, is revealed to be "some quality of mind they thought I possessed" (*I*, 26) rather than a specific skill in itself. Indeed, as the
streetwise Patel advises him shortly before the narrator departs for

Oxford, "all those books have made your head soft and rotten" (*I*, 240) and totally unfitted for the real world of commerce and economic success.

In effect, the novel undermines the narrator's narrow quest for book knowledge not by questioning the validity of this passport to success—access to language is a prime commodity for the immigrant (*I*, 123)—but by showing up the fallacy of its universal worth. *The Intended* demonstrates the relativity of knowledge, contextualizing its value and illustrating how much it is a construction of dominant discourse. Knowledge is not an attribute, but a matter of who thinks they have it and what kind others think you have. Further, it is often a matter of fantasy: the narrator's ostensibly superior knowledge of cricket is simply an ability to spin tall tales convincingly (*I*, 42). If any way of knowing is privileged in the text, it is that of the imagination, that of the artist, the storyteller. Thus, the West Indian facility for transforming the mundane into myth, as in the case of Peter's "insignificant" father who takes on "legendary proportions, transformed into hero and villain" (*I*, 56) or the drunken wreck, Richilo, made over by village stories into a degraded "prince" (*I*, 62), makes sense to the younger narrator in the way that Joseph's metaphysical musings on canonical literature (a different *way* of knowing) also do. This stress on the partiality of judgment, the inaccessible nature of truth as such, is intrinsic to the transcultural imagination and the narrative strategies of the bicultural works examined here.

I have suggested elsewhere that Phillips's *Cambridge* pursues a similar agenda to that of *The Intended* in its insistence that all wisdom is received, that the dominant discourse is a matter of the powerful deciding what the powerless should accept as given.[24] *Cambridge*, I maintain, questions the validity of historical truth by demonstrating its interested author-ity, its essential resemblance to fiction. However, I want to conclude this essay by mentioning yet another point of contact between *Cambridge* (and, indeed, all the novels examined) and *The Intended*: the refiguring of the middle passage, the voyage of discovery.

As noted, Dabydeen's novel is largely a retextualization of Conrad's *Heart of Darkness*. While the latter focuses on the journey from imperial center to colonial margin, the former reverses the voyage. In both, a hollow heart of darkness replaces expected fantasies. In the case of Dabydeen's text, the mother country is reduced to a cityscape of urban horror: "makeshift carts littered the Hill, stuffed with unsold cheap clothing, plastic goods, fruit and vegetables. Canals of filthy water trickled along the edge of the pavement and emptied into the gutter, the grills half-blocked by refuse and rotting vegetation. The prostitutes were already gathering in twos and threes, waiting for the Hill to empty and darkness to fall before coming out in full numbers" (*I,* 22). Apparently neutral description builds up, by sheer weight of negative associative items—"makeshift . . . littered . . . cheap . . . filthy . . . gutter . . . refuse . . . rotting . . . prostitutes . . . darkness"—into a gothic picture of decay at the center of Empire, with the creatures of the night just waiting to emerge from the shadows. How this contrasts with the alternative list of features associated with Englishness: "calm . . . grace . . . clarity . . . craftsmanship . . . china, coaches, period furniture, harpsichords, wigs" (*I,* 197)!

The journey in *The Intended* is at once physical—the narrator is always walking, traveling by bus, train, tube, not to mention his journeying from one continent to another—and textual: he moves imaginatively from this story into other remembered stories, both personal and canonical. So he cannot resist describing Patel's essay-writing strategy in terms of Wordsworth's dictum: "emotions recollected in the tranquillity of the examination room" (*I,* 11). Above all, the novel is pervaded by the trope of the middle passage, extended here to include the irreversible voyage of indentured Indian laborers to the West Indies. Again, a trivial trip on the Underground conjures up associations with other voyages:

> In the swift journey between Tooting Bec and Balham, we re-lived the passages from India to Britain, or India to the Caribbean to Britain, the long journeys of a previous century across unknown seas towards the shame of plantation labour; or the excitement with which we boarded *Air India* which died in a mixture of jet-lag, bewilderment and waiting in long queues in the immigration lounge at Heathrow—just like back home, the memory of beggars lining up outside a missionary church for a dollop of food from a white hand. (*I,* 17)

Who are the "we" with whom the narrating voice unproblematically identifies? Is it the ex-African slave population, with whom he identifies as his white girlfriend inspects his body, her purchase (*I,* 243)? Is it the "Asian diaspora" regrouped "in a South London schoolyard" (*I,* 5)? And if either, why the determined distancing from all groups? For this is insisted upon: of the boys in a particular home, he confides, "there were nine white, four black, and myself" (*I,* 81). Perhaps it is a West Indian Creole alliance he craves? But this too is problematized, as noted earlier, in his reluctance to be parceled up with *any* racial or national group in the eyes of the English. Like Lucy, he refuses ready-made and ultimately limiting notions of subjectivity; like Lucy, he opts for isolation as the ground of his protean and, as it turns out, textual self-creation; and like Lucy, he cannot help but situate this rewriting within a prescripted scenario of "angels masquerading as brutes" and vice versa. In other words, this impeccably postcolonial text always finds its matrix in relations of power.

A crucial section of the novel is an episode in which the narrator takes a summer job as attendant on a fun fair ride, a "World Cruise" boat trip along an underground canal, the tunnel wall of which "was decorated with painted scenes from various countries, in alphabetical order" (*I*, 76). The world's variety and cultural diversity is reduced, when the "magical" lights are switched off, to "smears of paint, crude in composition, lacking in artistry and beauty" (*I*, 77). Fixed categories of race and national provenance, not to mention a stereotypical view of received history, are presented for the entertainment of disinterested heirs of Empire who are more excited by the prospect of a quick sexual release, given "the relative darkness of the tunnel and the length of the ride, some fifteen minutes from beginning to end, in which they could obviously cast off superfluous clothing" (*I*, 77). Part of the narrator's duties involve scooping detritus from the previous night's customers out of the canal, and this provides a parodic account of the voyage of discovery which led to the inscription of various people and places on the wall of the tunnel, not to mention the presence of the narrator (through another set of journeys) in England. In a sense, the voyage of Conrad's *Heart of Darkness* also informs this section. Again, the allusion is parodic, as the air in the tunnel is "not so much brooding and mysterious as dank and still, the smell of unclean water filling my nostrils" (*I*, 77). Harvesting rubbish and discarded underclothes as he travels, the voyager reaches Africa:

> The scenes of Timbuktu . . . were depicted in harsh sunlight. There was a desert, some scorched trees, and five naked black men squatting or throwing spears after a zebra. They wore necklaces made out of the teeth of animals and each had a bone running through his nostrils. A black woman with full breasts and gleaming thighs carried a pot on her head. Another sat on a donkey so oddly—her buttocks merged into its flank— that it seemed she was having some kind of bizarre sex with it. (*I*, 78)

It is all here: primitivism, savagery, poverty and natural depletion, sexual excess, depravity. Conrad's inscription of Africa is taken to extremes here, history and cultural contact trivialized, and the result of the voyage is a set of colonial caricatures. Further, this tableau is overwritten by racist and obscene graffiti scrawled on the body of the black woman, finally altered again by the narrator's embarrassed clean up job. It seems to me that what Dabydeen is positing in this joke knowledge of the Other, set in a dank and sleazy cityscape, is that the real heart of darkness lies right at the heart of Empire. The underground voyage, which for many patrons is hardly above board, is a mockery: those who embark never see other cultures, only caricatures of what is already known via a chain of textual inscriptions, reaching their nadir here in the crude stereotypes inscribed on the wall. As Kincaid demonstrates in *A Small Place*, tourists who journey for pleasure never really embark on a voyage of discovery.

It is noticeable that Guyana does not figure among the representations of the World Cruise. Yet it is a center of sorts in the text. Given the corruption, the filth, the debased nature of the heart of Empire which the narrator faithfully records, the text itself chronicles yet another middle passage. The narrator's desire to escape the shame of his underprivileged past (imaged, as in Naipaul's *A House for Mr. Biswas*, in terms of disorder and jumble) and the shame of contemporary urban Britain—founded, as Patel proves, on drugs, pornography, and exploitation (*I*, 241)—initiates a series of remembrances that take him back home. For as the narrator's grandmother tells him, "Englan far away like India" (*I*, 67). What he carries within him during his journeying is a gift, like that given him by Auntie Clarice before his first departure from the West Indies:

> "Tek some [plums] to Englan and when you see white man give him and say you Auntie Clarice send him gift from she back garden in Albion Village, Berbice, Guyana, South America, all the way across the Ocean. . . . and that he and he race must be kind to you and we, for all body on dis earth is one God's people, not true?" (*I*, 39)

The narrator's gift, which causes him much suffering, is the transcultural imagination that constantly, and with varying degrees of self-consciousness, bridges worlds or, to use Walcott's image, stitches horizons together. The stereoscopic vision entailed necessitates a struggle for a form that eludes iron-bar language in order to creatively decipher the links and contradictions between cultures and peoples.

If *Omeros* closes with an assertion of epic truths about human nature as played out among St. Lucian fishermen and displaced expatriates who have finally found a home, *The Intended* ends with another departure that signals a further dissolution of the narrator's protean identity. It chronicles the plight (in this case, the flight) of those who live *between* places, with only a confused knowledge of ancestry and origins, but aware that the alternative "idea of England" is fantasy. The choices lie in accepting oneself as nothing, a big zero (as does Joseph), or assimilation, the narrator's goal (*I*, 56), or an (in this case, textual) attempt to find a home in the gaps between. If *Omeros* is imbued with the belief that "all body on dis earth is one God's people," *The Intended* stresses the provisional nature of all identity. Like the other texts discussed, Dabydeen's demonstrates the constructedness of knowledge and truth, in the process breaking down hierarchical value systems that seek to place people in terms of oppositions like subject/object, oppressor/oppressed, conqueror/victim, angel/brute, insider/outsider. The dual pull between retaining cultural specificity and the desire to integrate, complicates notions of home in these bicultural works so that a constant movement—between past and present, the Caribbean and the metropolis, inner and outer experience—repeatedly rehearses the middle passage, rewriting it each time round. If indeed the protagonists in the novels of Naipaul, Kincaid, Dabydeen, and Phillips are at home anywhere, it is precisely in the ongoing journey of the text. As Walcott puts it, there are "two journeys / in every odyssey": one through space and time, and one internal; one by ship or plane, and one on paper.[25]

Hulme, in his inquiry into the question of West Indianness, favors an approach which "does not involve some kind of nationality test which writers have to pass to qualify for admission: books belong to Caribbean or West Indian literature if they have dealings with that area" ("P," 6). In this essay, I have suggested that one development in the literature is the number of texts in the last decade or so which have dealings not only with that area but with other areas as well, texts that site their narratives in voyages of discovery between areas, connecting all shores. Increasingly, it seems to me, the condition of betweenity has become an important focus in Caribbean literature and criticism. And that the trend to bicultural cross-fertilization is noticeable in popular culture is beyond question: witness Apache Indian, Birmingham deejay of Indian origin, who welds Jamaican dancehall and Indian musical influences with African American rap; or Maxi Priest, whose smooth English-based lovers rock is juxtaposed with Shabba Ranks's raw dancehall chanting. Perhaps Best is right, and this betweenity is a vital resource for us on the journey into the twenty-first century.

I want to end with reference to Erna Brodber's *Louisiana*. Here is a West Indian novel set entirely in the United States, written by someone whose base has been incontrovertibly Jamaican. And yet the text conforms magically to what I have been calling, variously, the transcultural or bicultural (and, others may add, diasporic) imagination, and epitomizes the stereoscopic vision. Ella, the African American protagonist (I use the term with reservations, for like all Brodber's work, the communal nature of the narrative project is distinctive), Ella, whose ancestry is Jamaican, is engaged in an anthropological study of black folk culture in Louisiana. Through several communicative media, she accesses voices which convince her "that the nature or extent of the influence of black America on the Caribbean and vice versa has [not] been explored as it should."[26] This bald summary does little justice to the complex nature of the narrative means by which an alternative way of seeing is arrived at, one which valorizes betweenity as a space where the tyrannic authority of Western scientific, phallogocentric discourse is neither subverted, refuted, or really acknowledged with more than a passing nod; instead, it is shown to be unequal to the task of interpretation. What emerges from this text is a belief that the old metaphysics cannot, any longer, apply without deathliness, without zombification.

Postcolonial theory suggests attention to the literary text as theoretical paradigm. In this, *Louisiana* is exemplary. For what the narrative conveys is a model by which victim status is bypassed; the entire discursive apparatus through which alterity becomes normative is rejected. Ella is advised by different reasoning voices that "enough of her line had been wasted in battle, and that she should take a new approach to fighting" (*L*, 155). And that approach, like Walcott's, involves "wanting to pull the sides of the sea together, wanting to sew them little islands together and tack them on to New Orleans" (*L*, 148). Another historical vision, this; without dismissing cultural specificity, it makes use of buried knowledge, spirit work, and, above all, migration of the imagination, sea-swiftlike, to write *other* important voyages and passages into the ever-widening range of West Indian cultural signification. And the result? I would say that the result is a signpost to healing, a healing of what Walcott calls—and all West Indian writing addresses—"the rift in the soul."

Notes

1. Peter Hulme, "The Place of *Wide Sargasso Sea*," *Wasafiri* 20 (Autumn 1994): 5. Hereafter "P," cited in the text.

2. Kenneth Ramchand, "*Wide Sargasso Sea*," in Pierrette M. Frickey, ed., *Critical Perspectives on Jean Rhys* (Washington: Three Continents Press, 1990), 194. Hulme notes that this commentary is reprinted from Ramchand's *An Introduction to the Study of West Indian Literature* (1980).

3. Susheila Nasta, "Editorial: The Scramble for New Literatures," *Wasafiri* 20 (Autumn 1994): 3. Hereafter "E," cited in the text.

4. Pico Iyer, "The Empire Writes Back," *Time Magazine*, 8 February 1989, 46. Hereafter "EWB," cited in the text.

5. Diana Brydon and Helen Tiffin, *Decolonising Fictions* (Mundelstrup: Dangaroo Press, 1993), 24. Hereafter *DF*, cited in the text.

6. Chris Tiffin and Alan Lawson, eds., *De-Scribing Empire: Post-colonialism and Textuality* (London: Routledge, 1994), 233. Hereafter *DE*, cited in the text.

7. In popular music, this kind of playing with doubleness is common: as a random example, consider Ini Kamoze's 1995 dancehall hit, where the "hot-stepper" (heart-stopper/upsetter?) unproblematically declares himself "a lyrical gangster," where the refrain "murderer!" is followed by the line, "Still love you like that!"

8. The reference is to Bill Ashcroft, as quoted in "Constitutive Graphonomy: A Post-colonial Theory of Literary Writing," *Kunapipi* 11, no. 1 (1989): 58–79.

9. V. S. Naipaul, *The Enigma of Arrival: A Novel* (New York: Viking Penguin, 1987). Hereafter *E*, cited in the text.

10. Rob Nixon, *London Calling: V. S. Naipaul, Postcolonial Mandarin* (Oxford: Oxford University Press, 1991), 6. Hereafter *LC*, cited in the text.

11. Mark McWatt, "The West Indian Writer and the Self: Recent 'Fictional' Autobiography by Naipaul and Harris," *Journal of West Indian Literature* 3, no. 1 (January 1989): 16–27. Hereafter "WIWS," cited in the text.

12. David Streitfeld, "The Unflinching Gaze of V. S. Naipaul," *The Washington Post*, 12 April 1989, B2, B3.

13. Helen Tiffin, "Rites of Resistance: Counter-Discourse and West Indian Biography," *Journal of West Indian Literature* 3, no. 1 (January 1989): 39. Hereafter "RR," cited in the text.

14. Jamaica Kincaid, *Lucy* (New York: Farrar Straus Giroux, 1990), 4. Hereafter *L*, cited in the text.

15. Patricia Harkins, " 'Masquerading as Angels' : Masking and Unmasking in Jamaica Kincaid's *Lucy*" (paper presented at the tenth annual Conference on West Indian Literature, University of the West Indies, St. Augustine, Trinidad, June 5–7, 1991).

16. Selwyn Cudjoe, "Jamaica Kincaid and the Modernist Project," *Caribbean Women Writers: Proceedings of the First International Conference*, ed. Selwyn Cudjoe (Wellesley, Mass.: Calaloux, 1990), 215–32.

17. Karen King-Aribasala, " 'Columbus in Chains': The Voyage as a Cultural Crossing: An Analysis of Jamaica Kincaid's *Lucy*" (paper presented at the ninth Triennial Conference of ACLALS, University of the West Indies, Mona, Jamaica, August 13–20, 1992), 10. Hereafter "CC," cited in the text.

18. Alison Donnell, "Cultural Ambivalence and the Unravelling of Anglo-Centric Narratives in Jamaica Kincaid's Fiction" (paper presented at the ninth Triennial Conference of ACLALS, University of the West Indies, Mona, Jamaica, August 13–20, 1992).

19. " 'I use a cut and slash policy of writing': Jamaica Kincaid Talks to Gerhard Dilger," *Wasafiri* 18 (Autumn 1992): 21. Hereafter "I," cited in the text.

20. Pamela Buchanan Muirhead, "An Interview with Jamaica Kincaid," *Clockwatch Review* 9, nos. 1–2 (1994–1995): 45.

21. Mark McWatt, "The Loneliness of the Long-Distance Writer: Exile and the Trans-Cultural Imagination in Guyanese Novelists" (paper presented at the eleventh annual Conference on West Indian Literature, University of Guyana, Turkeyen Campus, Georgetown, May 1992), 1. Hereafter "L," cited in the text.

22. David Dabydeen, *The Intended* (London: Secker & Warburg, 1991), 197. Hereafter *I*, cited in the text.

23. This list is, it seems to me, an allusion to Kamau Brathwaite's nursery rhyme catalogue of "things English" in his poem "Calypso," in *The Arrivants: A New World Trilogy* (Oxford: Oxford University Press, 1981), 48:

> And of course it was a wonderful time . . .
> when captains carried receipts for rices
> letters spices wigs
> opera glasses swaggering asses
> debtors vices pigs.

The effect in the poem, as in Dabydeen's text, is bathetic, undermining the grandeur of the so-called glory days of Empire.

24. Evelyn O'Callaghan, "Historical Fiction and Fictional History: Caryl Phillips's *Cambridge*," *Journal of Commonwealth Literature* 29, no. 2 (1993): 34–47.

25. Derek Walcott, *Omeros* (Boston: Faber, 1990), 291.

26. Erna Brodber, *Louisiana* (London and Port of Spain: New Beacon, 1994), 154; cited as *L* in the following discussion.

Transitional Identities: Haiti, the Caribbean, and the "Black Atlantic"

Eddy Souffrant
Marquette University

The Story of Collective Identity

IN this essay I argue that for the most part concepts of identity are negative, and ethnic identity, for example, provides a usefully illustrative starting point. African American identity, or Haitian identity, or Caribbean identity, or any other kind of identity whatsoever might be understood as an example of an identity imposed directly or indirectly on some group. And to the extent that the identity is imposed, it is not an authentic expression of a self free of external influences. It is a response, and as such constitutes a negative exercise. But whether a response or not, any assertion of a categorical identity is always an exclusion; in some cases it is an exclusion of others and in other cases it is an exclusion of other options or possibilities of being. Many versions of ethnic and gender identity, for example, participate in this sort of exclusion. This sense of identity constructed by means of exclusion is as much a negative identity formation as the first, for by its positive assertion, it excludes others by making specific the criteria of membership. We can also observe that in some of these identity-forming activities, some "straw group" is constructed, and that group's assets or peculiarities or idiosyncrasies are contrasted with the privileged group's own supposed positive aspects.

Thus, conceptions of identity, given the above proposal, are formulated against a background of exclusion. The suggested second sense of identity addressed above is a response to exclusiveness and from this response an image of the self, or the group to which one is believed to belong, is developed. In addition to the above two types of conceptions of identity, a third type of identity formation is possible. This third type of identity formation is the most attractive kind, for it speaks to a descriptiveness which appears to do away with the handicaps of negative constructions of identity. It seems to need no crutches to assert itself, for presumably that identity is reflected in the unique descriptive histories of groups. Thus, for example, we speak of the jazz of African America, the steel drums of Trinidad, the reggae of Jamaica, the bossa nova of Brazil, the compas of Haiti. In these assignments of properties, the ingenuity and uniqueness of the group referenced seems to take precedence over the difficulties of exclusion experienced by members of the group. In this way one might suggest that some conceptions of identity are positive conceptions. They are not dependent upon hegemonic forces that may have shaped those conceptions of identity. One might thus argue that a negative conception of identity is no longer warranted and that all groups, despite their plight, do surmount their circumstances to present a uniqueness which truly represents their true selves. But as I will argue further, even such conceptions of identity are problematic, for they serve to narrow the range of a group's identity by presuming, on the one hand, property over this or that expression or, on the other, by preventing, in its determination of descriptive strength, alternative expressions of uniqueness.

Modernity and the African American Response

Let us consider the role of African American experience and the philosophy that ensued from that experience as an identity-forming project. African American philosophy, we know, is a recent development in the field of philosophy and according to Cornel West, it is a welcome addition to the subject matter. The reason is simple. In West's analysis, we gather that a vitally important space is offered the African American philosopher. The latter's task does not only consist in the maintenance of the activities of the field of philosophy, but also in providing adequate response to the hasty call in some quarters for the demise of philosophy. The call for the end of philosophy is premature, according to West, and his analysis determines first, the way in which the call for the end of philosophy crept into our psyche and second, why African American philosophy may yield both the restoration of the field and the resolution of the anguish expressed by the call. For West, a crucial moment in the development of modern philosophy consists in the withdrawal of philosophy from sociopolitical activities. If the impotence of philosophy, as seen from the perspective of the moderns, is to be corrected, then a reincorporation of the sociopolitical into philosophical discourse is necessary. African American philosophy and its philosophers are, in West's view, uniquely placed to execute such reincorporation.

Such reincorporation is vital since, to the extent that philosophy is conceived as an alienated discourse with the promise of yielding truth independently of the sociopolitical environment, it will, if this truth is really inaccessible, serve no purpose at all when alternative instruments of inquiry are more readily available and more precise than philosophy itself is. If philosophy cannot provide answers to the socioeconomic difficulties of our time, the irrelevance of the field is almost assured. With this thought in mind, a couple of issues need to be kept in view. The first is whether philosophy or any other field of study is or was ever truly independent of the socioeconomic environment. The second issue is whether there is an alternative conception of philosophy, an alternative development in the field, that would speak to the shortsightedness of the call for the end of philosophy.

West engages the second view. From his perspective, the developments in the history of philosophy show a progress from modern philosophy to the present that firmly places the presence of African American philosophy in the tradition exemplified by philosophers such as Descartes, Dewey, Kant, Hegel, Locke, Hume, and Marx. African American philosophy, in contrast to what might be called broadly European "Old World" philosophy, uses as its data of inquiry the contemporary circumstances of African Americans. African American philosophy speaks to the intimate engagement of persons and fields of study, to the interdisciplinary aspects of inquiry, to the inextricable link of philosophy to "politics and power—to structures of domination and mechanisms of control."[1]

But why should we seriously consider power and politics in the march of philosophy? There are at least two fundamental reasons why these might be reintroduced as constituents of philosophical thinking. The first is that the history of philosophy has systematically alienated the workings of groups as both makers of history and potential influences on individuals. The second reason is that politics and other structures of power, as expressions of the manner in which individuals are influenced by the social environment, have historically drawn upon expressions of philosophical systems and theories of persons and their environments. Thus, to the extent that individuals are lodged in social environments and that interaction between the social and the individual is neglected, there is room for an alternative approach to the role and study of philosophy. And furthermore, to the extent that philosophical inquiry leaves unexamined specific expressions of the manner in which the social and the individual interact, a renewed role for philosophers is required.

This proposed intuition motivates West's article. He believes that the African American philosopher may uniquely contribute to the unmasking of social structures of domination and control. Two passages in his article highlight, in my view, the unique position of philosophy and the role of the African American philosopher. He first suggests the problematic of contemporary philosophy in an assessment of the contemporary world and the latter's challenge to philosophy and its workers:

> A sense of reaching an historical dead end with no foreseeable way out and no discernible liberating projects or even credible visions in the near future . . . pervades the present and the dominant forms of intellectual activity, especially philosophical reflection, enact this sense of impotence: analytical philosophy makes a fetish of technical virtuosity and uses it as a measure to regulate the intense careerism in the profession; anti-academic professional avant-gardists fiercely assault fellow colleagues and fervently attack notions of epistemological privilege, yet remain relatively silent about racial, sexual, and class privilege in society at large; and poststructuralists perennially decenter prevailing discourses and dismantle philosophical and literary texts, yet valorize a barren, ironic disposition by deconstructing, hence disarming and discarding, any serious talk about praxis. ("PPP," 56)

West's concern is that critiques of the postphilosophical present reject the notion of academic or intellectual (epistemological) privilege harbored by analytical philosophers, while remaining oblivious to the many instantiations of sociopolitical privilege. And when they move to question these latter privileges, they overlook the relevance of the lived. It is in the observance of this silence that the African American philosopher's task is made explicit. West argues that:

> The principal task of the Afro-American philosopher is to keep alive the idea of a revolutionary future, a better future different from the deplorable present, a state of affairs in which the multifaceted oppression of Afro-Americans (and others) is, if not eliminated, alleviated. Therefore the Afro-American philosopher must preserve the crucial Hegelian (and deeply Christian) notions of negation and transformation of what is in light of revolutionary not-yet. The notions of negation and transformation . . . promote the activity of resistance to what is and elevate the praxis of struggle against existing realities. ("PPP," 57)

West determines that the major project of the "Afro-American philosopher" must consist in her being aware of her presence in the field, understanding the philosophical past, avoiding its shortcomings of presuming ahistoricity, and engaging in a negation and transformation of the present. In my interpretation of West's view, Afro-American philosophy engages its practitioner in the problematic of the philosophical tradition inherited from the moderns. The articulation of this problematic asks whether philosophy can be exercised from without the social.

Hegel's solution in identifying the historical rather than the autonomous individual in philosophy (see *Reason in History*) is a first attempt at the resolution of the problematic. Marx's offer to consider a particular system of alienation, capitalism, paved the way for future analyses of structures of domination. The African American in his practices under specific forms of oppression is for West a testament to the potential antinihilist futures of a revolutionary posture. The church, jazz, tap-dancing, funk, rap, gospel choir are all expressions of that disposition. But in addition they are, in my mind, examples of the future open to liberation movements and they constitute the multifarious expressions found in the "prophetic" outcome to which West refers.

Prophetic outcomes of liberation movements are not predetermined. The African American cannot deny his history in the Americas, nor the legacy of slavery, colonization, and racism on the American psyche and on America's sociopolitical structures. In this reality, the African in the Americas is locked into a particular vision of this legacy's presence in the American environment and is constrained in the range of her potential contribution to that environment. But the diversity of individual answers to the American experience suggests that although locked into a flow of history, the prophetic thrust toward a solution to the structures of domination have exhibited themselves in particularly unique fashions among members of the African American community. Paradoxically, the very response to a common cause of oppression, the diversity constitutive of the African American response, prevents us from acknowledging categorically that there be a positively discernible African American identity. This difficulty may in the end be the very difficulty of the contemporary movement in philosophy emanating from the modern tradition. For while the modern tradition sought to give meaning and to yield the certain identity of the world about us, it did not, perhaps until the advent of Kantian philosophy (see *Critique of Pure Reason*), awake from the "dogmatic slumber" which prevents the realization that truth and certainty are anthropomorphic and that although access to them is available to all by force of human constitution, a freedom is available to individuals as each apprehends the world in his or her peculiar manner. Beyond the metaphysical claims of a human nature, i.e., a common group identity, such an identity is hard to gauge in actual sociopolitical settings.

Political and National Identity: The Legacy of Modernity

Consider an interesting example of the problem of identity. The country of Colombia publishes a list of countries whose citizens, if they wish to visit that country, are required to have government approval from the prospective host country. Citizens of Haiti, The Dominican Republic, China, Cuba, and several other countries on that list are expected to prove good health, economic solvency, legitimacy of invitation to visit Colombia, etc.[2] Curiously, not found on this list are countries like France whose imposing policies, for example, impact nefariously on the peoples of Togo, Algeria, and the Middle East in general; the United States whose contemporary foreign policies and history have been less than altruistic; the Soviet Union, Germany, Israel, Portugal, Spain, Belgium, etc. No reason is forwarded as to why the citizens of the clearly targeted countries are to show more proof of acceptability in order to enter Colombia than those of the countries whose global and/or domestic histories can, with little effort, be shown to have helped eliminate large numbers of the members of presumably antagonistic racial, ethnic, and political groups.

The countries whose citizens are directly targeted in the Colombian list are represented as more repugnant, as having qualities less consistent with Colombian national identity, than those nations who have traditionally functioned as hegemonic global powers. A Haitian identity, for example, again if it were contingent on that list, might lead a member of Haitian society to self-doubt or worse to self-denigration. For either one is truly a freak, at least according to the moral, medical, and global standards implied by the nature of the listing, or perhaps in the case of the Caribbean countries, one is excluded on the basis of not participating properly or fully in some presumed "Caribbean identity formation." I should like, however, to present the following: that the very phrase or concept of a "Caribbean identity" is itself a paradox. To speak of a Caribbean identity without taking into consideration an analysis of the structures of domination, be they political or economic that may compel one to yearn for that identity, is to overlook the reality of identity formation in the contemporary world. But what is it that constitutes such claims of identity, as in say, Caribbean identity?

A few years ago in 1993, we witnessed the implementation of a consensus expressed in the very Charter of the Organization of American States that in American nation-states representative democracy ought to be the primary mode of government and that the purpose of the OAS should be to promote and strengthen these representative democracies. But from 1948 (the year of the formal establishment of the OAS) to 1959 when the "Meeting of the Consultation of Ministers of Foreign Affairs" adopted the "Declaration of Santiago," the OAS in effect reiterated its commitment to representative government as it asserted the incongruency of democracy and the exercise of power by dictators or oligarchs.[3] This general attitude vis-à-vis the proper exercise of power expressed in the charter and reinforced by the Declaration of Santiago was further strengthened in 1991 by the "Santiago Commitment to Democracy and a resolution on representative democracy."[4] The resolution asserts that the Permanent Council of the OAS will automatically convene a meeting to examine the situation and decide on the courses to follow, whenever democratic (thus legitimate) exercises of power are suddenly interrupted in any of the OAS member states.

In Haiti, the coup d'état against the elected government of Jean-Bertrand Aristide in September of 1991 put the OAS resolution to the test. In a subsequent meeting of the Ministers of Foreign Affairs, a resolution was adopted to isolate Haiti from the rest of the OAS states and, indeed, the world at large. As we concern ourselves with questions of identity, we might begin by considering whether we could glean some aspects of a Haitian identity based in part on the story told thus far. Furthermore, can a view of a Caribbean identity be likewise gotten from the sketch offered here? Certainly one might draw from the preceding presentation that a democratic government is the appropriate one for the member states of the OAS. The view that democracy be the agreed-upon mode of exercised government and that transgression of that mode be duly punished might be construed as an assertion of a common political identity imposed upon OAS member states. Thus, we might do well to look first at the impact of the presumption of legitimacy, derived from a certain form of governance, and asserted upon a presumed collective Haitian identity.

Haitian Identity

Any conception of a Haitian identity based on the history of Haiti in the international context would constitute a negative identity.

The OAS resolution imputes a vision of the Haitian country and its people that appears to fall into two general categories. One category would suggest that Haitians as a whole, that is to say their collective identity, by its support of the coup, renders Haitian identity internationally delinquent and therefore deserving of isolation. The other more sympathetic reading would suggest that the conflict between government and people, precipitating a coup, might indicate conflicting strategies of Haitian identity construction and thus require some deeper reading of these competing identity claims. In either case, the OAS stricture of democracy might be seen to limit the possibilities of alternative modalities of Haitian identity construction. Here the dominant context is democracy, a particular and fixed political mode of identity asserted on Haiti and the Caribbean OAS group. Thus, alternative identity politics are obliterated. Haiti, however, as a physical entity in the Caribbean, cannot simply be obliterated. As a body politic with physical, national, cultural, and historical integrity, it has to be whipped into shape whether as a rogue or as a democratically retarded nation. The structures of identity are already established and no alternative notions are deemed viable. For example, any argument for the restoration of a Haitian viability tends typically to disintegrate into a debate about recalcitrance and suggestions that the Haitian leaders are not acquiescing or are rather reluctantly adhering to international accords. Short of the preceding type of polemical dialogues, one could very well opt for the kind of vision that Michel Rolph Trouillot might propose.

From Trouillot's perspective, Haitian identity does not respond directly to the issue of whether or not Haiti is a political anomaly in the Caribbean or the Americas.[5] His contribution to the question of identity is in providing first an interpretation of history that suggests that the historical narrative is a bundle of silence. As such, from his view one gathers that to develop a conception of Haitian history without an understanding of the relationships among the historical circumstances that lead to the present would constitute an incomplete history. Another value of this contribution is in its pointing out that a narrative of Haitian identity based on contemporary political fads does a disservice to Haitian integrity and historicity. For given the interpretation offered earlier, if the isolation of Haiti is based on its refusal to partake in an ideal of democratic identity presumably shared by all the member states of the OAS, the isolation robs Haiti of an integrity displayed in the march of its own historical legacy. Thus any narrative of Haiti that would not engage a dialogue making clear the internal complexities of the country and its inhabitants would be severely flawed.

The history of political philosophy has for some time concerned itself with the justification of government, of determining who should govern (Aristotle and Plato), how broadly the coercion of government should extend (Hobbes, Locke, Rousseau), and whether limits ought to be imposed on the freedom of individuals and what it is that constitutes that freedom (Marx, Kant, Mill). The international response to the Haitian situation has highlighted in my mind the recent focus of political philosophy on questions of representations, that is to say, on issues of the proper exercise of power. This shift in focus speaks to the diminished concern for the justification of governmental entities, expressed in the contemporary period of cold-war struggles, in favor of an assessment of the manner in which power is exercised or delegated. This concern helps to explain the attention given to democratization processes the world over. Haiti's significance in the international community was poignant for this latter purpose; its international identity, therefore, was based largely on this recent pattern in political philosophy.

Haiti and the General Problem of Identity

The problem of collective identity given the Haitian case is manifold. Identity, if we are to presume some relevance vis-à-vis the Caribbean or the Americas, is fundamentally negative. Given the initial isolation by the international community, Haitian collective identity would seek to defend or counter such an isolation. Internationally, one is either a rogue or a work in progress, some distance behind a number of other democratic works in progress. The recent management of Haiti by international forces seems to point to the idea of Haiti as international rogue. But as I have proposed above, such a limited representation seems to speak more about the inadequacies of an imposed democratic governance structure on the complexities of Haiti than about Haitian identity formation. Democracy is a source of collective identity, but it yields a political identity. As a source of political identity, it is by no means the only source of collective identity. However, if a group, whether national or international, has deemed it the appropriate expression of its identity, then internal dissentions or attempts to gain exemption from such collective identity produces either recalcitrant members or misfits. Such renegade members can be redirected, coached to reenter the democratic world, or suffer exclusion from membership until compliance and conformity are restored.[6] What is it about democracy that makes it appealing to engage in such unquestionably coercive conformity at both the national and global level?

Contemporary Democracies

The almost obsessive attachment to democracy as a global phenomenon or as a criterion of proper international behavior is, from my perspective, a recent wave in the conception of governance. The development of political philosophy has witnessed a shift. We have slowly, but radically, moved from perspectives concerned with justifying the presence of authority to another concern, one where questions of, Who should govern and how? are significant. It is not strange at all that Hobbes, Locke, Rousseau, Marx, Mill (the younger), Bentham, and other political philosophers have tried to supply us with conceptions or criteria by which to determine the acceptability of a coercive force within the socioeconomic realm.

These political philosophers have suggested that a justified government is one where the viability of individuals is respected, supported, enhanced or simply maintained. Democratic governance, whether in its representative Hobbesian form or its authoritarian Aristotelian version, has sought to convince us of why power in the public realm is acceptable. Recent developments in political philosophy, however, arguably best exemplified in the works of Robert Dahl, have attempted to refocus our attention away from concerns with justified governance (here the belief is that a democracy is "a necessary condition for the best political order"[7]) to concentrate on effective modes of governance, that is to say, the effective exercise of power. So we have moved from the claim that a justified government is democratic to the issue of how to exercise power within a democracy.

The logic of governance compels one to presume a constituency. Democracy provides an answer to the question of what to do with a perceived constituency. A perceived constituency without an identity is a renegade. It must be controlled and given an identity. From the logic of governance which necessitates a constituency, we gather identity. Identity given this perspective is an attempt to make a coherence, to make a collective of a perceived constituency. My argument thus far suggests that justification of power and the exercise of power are therefore relevant only to the extent that a constituency can be produced and identified. Thus, collective identity is superficial, and when it serves the attempt to form a constituency, collective identity is exclusionary at best and at worst, it is ephemeral. Indeed, collective democratic identity is as ephemeral as the concept of identity itself.

Political Identity Revisited

Issues of ethnicity, race, and gender, as well as issues of sexual predilections, age, economic or social class appurtenances, etc., are significant components of identity. They are as crucial as the political belongingness yielded by citizenship. One might therefore suggest that challenges faced by American, Brazilian, French, British, and German democracies, for example, are in large part the results of the peculiar difficulties posed to contemporary democracies by trans/supranationalisms or diasporic identities. Identity discourses thus come in different forms. The concept of identity proposed by thinkers such as Dahl, for example, is one that is strongly negative. It is negative in both its formulation and in its practical and theoretical ramifications. Such negative identity formulations are opposed to strategies of self-identification which offer the possibility of relinquishing the limitations of the collective identity processes.

Contact Identities

The foregoing has been an attempt to disabuse us of the belief that collective identity is fundamentally political. Perhaps it is true, after all, that political participation, or governance generally, is a luxury of the elite. For when we accept the suggestions of Dahl, for example, that concerns of alterity can be overcome by procedural and pluralistic means, we have accepted the primacy of the political and are thus tempted to accept, as Dahl does, that struggles of autonomy are struggles of the political. In contrast to such a proposal, let us consider, for example, the struggle for gender and ethnic identities within American democracy.

Identity is negative transition; it is a negative imposition on one's positive contribution to an environment. Is there an alternative means for contribution without this negative transition? In this regard, the earlier discussion regarding the challenges for African American philosophical discourse is instructive. West reminds us that by taking the experiential seriously, African American philosophy has been able to produce a body of work by drawing upon African American experience. One aspect of African American philosophy concerned itself with determining the extent to which blacks were or were not problems on the American sociopolitical land-scape. In their own ways, thinkers such as W. E. B. DuBois and Booker T. Washington, for example, justified African American presence and experience in the American landscape by arguing that the African American experience was generally reflective of issues relevant to all Americans. Through analyses such as DuBois's and Washington's we were reminded that the particularities of African American experience in the American landscape was historically linked to an intersection of racial ideologies and economic policies. This nexus of race and economics was an equation produced at the expense of the person of African descent, transplanted to American soil.

The exclusionary practices consequent on the intersection of ra-cial ideology and economic policy kept the African American from full participation in American society. Hazel Carby, for example, has reflected on the exclusionary practices which served, inter alia, to frustrate African American identity construction. In her analysis of the Columbian Exposition in Chicago in 1893, as well as in her dis-cussion of the general status of blacks in the U.S., Carby indicates that the black women who spoke at the World's Congress of Repre-sentative Women were seen more as a reflection of the theme of ex-oticism which pervaded the fair than they were understood to be true representatives of harmony among women regardless of race.[8]

Carby argues that the strategies of exclusion grounded in race were hostile to African American women's attempts to represent themselves as significant contributors and agents in American soci-ety. The "cult of true womanhood"[9] worked to place the African American woman in a precarious position. If the cult of true woman-hood is to be believed, then the true woman is not black:

> The discourse of true womanhood was bound by a shared social under-standing that external physical appearance reflected internal qualities of character and therefore provided an easily discernible indicator of the function of a female of the human species . . . Strength and ability to bear fatigue, argued to be so distasteful a presence in a white woman, were positive features to be emphasized in the promotion and selling of a black female field hand . . . [Therefore, black] women were not represented as of the same order of being as their mistresses; they lacked the physical, external evidence of the presence of a pure soul. (*RW*, 25–26)

The ideology of "true womanhood" locked white women within the confines of patriarchal limitations of gender. They were the "weaker sex." The ideology simultaneously delimited the participation of black women within the category of "woman" since they were, at best, degraded examples of such a category. The ideology thus maintained not only the sexism but also the racist tendencies of the wider society. Thus, although the women's movement had, at that juncture, begun to develop an image of womanhood other than that which was imposed by patriarchy, to the extent that its critique left racism untouched, the movement sought its advancement at the expense of black people, generally, and black women in particular.

Paul Gilroy and Contact Identity

In her analyses of identity constructions within the early development of the women's movement, Carby draws our attention to strategic weaknesses and contradictions which speak, yet again, of the problematic nature of collective identity. Limiting and limited despite its various guises, as an alternative to collective identity formations, let us consider the possibility of contact identity, and in this regard, the work of Paul Gilroy is instructive. Gilroy argues that attempts to maintain an integral identity whether based on culture or nationality are bound to encounter, in the Americas and Europe, the problem of the "black Atlantic." As Gilroy states:

> The contemporary black arts movement in film, visual arts, and theater as well as music . . . has created a new topography of loyalty and identity in which the structures and presuppositions of the nation-state have been left behind because they are seen to be outmoded . . . Columbus's pilot, Pedro Nino, was also an African. The history of the black Atlantic since then, continually crisscrossed by the movements of black people— not only as commodities but engaged in various struggles towards emancipation, autonomy, and citizenship—provides a means to reexamine the problems of nationality, location, identity, and historical memory. They all emerge from it with special clarity if we contrast the national, nationalistic, and ethnically absolute paradigms of cultural criticism to be found in England and America with those hidden expressions, both residual and emergent, that attempt to be global or outer-national in nature.[10]

Gilroy is among a number of thinkers who argue that the legacy of modernity consists in our adherence to conceptions of valued differences.[11] In response to such alienating categorizations, the postmodernist trend has been to explode the inherently binary oppositions of the identity discussions of the moderns in exchange for a multiplicity of cohabiting identities within an identifiable container—like the nation-state.

Gilroy's use of the image of the ship as a dislocating agent is informative for our discussion of identity. In the foregoing discussions, we have realized that the political does not exhaust the conception of identity. In the brief discussion of the African American situation, for example, we sense an appeal for identity based on the daily contact and histories of individuals as well as groups. It is this sense of the quotidian and the interactions and contacts among persons that has motivated Gilroy's work. He realizes that with the nation-state as instrument, governance has remained an organized exercise with an aim to control. One need only gloss the literature of politics to note that governance has always understood its goals as the control of the constituency, the control of violence, the security of the propertied class, etc. And even in its most recent guise of global democracy, the aim continues to be control, but now it is an effort to neutralize demographic and technological transnational forces.

The black Atlantic, in its numerous manifestations, unravels these modernist and postmodernist dispositions. The image of the ship in Gilroy's work therefore serves two purposes. It provides a space where articulation with the Other, whether at the interpersonal level or with the group, can be explored. Second, it is a motif for the middle passage, a motif which therefore links the slave trade to its profound influences on industrialization and modernization. Thus, Gilroy's deployment of the motif of the ship serves to remind us that modernity, as a conceptual framework, and modernization, as the actual outcome of that framework, cannot be divorced from either the particular or general contributions of blacks. And if one cannot deny the presence of blacks in an otherwise presumably exclusive white tradition of progress and achievement, we are logically brought to the inevitability of "mestizaje," "métissage," "mulatrisme," "créolisation," "hybridity."

Of course, there is little wonder that when faced with such dogged arguments of purity and exclusion, individuals such as DuBois and Frantz Fanon experience the "double-consciousness" whose constituents they have shared with us through their respective analyses of the problem of identity. The double-consciousness, one may recall, is a pathology. It is a pathology, in large part, because these intellectuals themselves experienced and critiqued the schizophrenic doubleness of their own existence. They were excluded as fully participating members of their respective societies on the basis of a spurious purity which they would have presumably sullied if they had been permitted to partake in the life of the state at the same level as their putative co-citizens. Yet the reality which they experienced and critiqued had profound value not only for themselves or others like them, but indeed for the entire society in which each individual had his existence. Their individual experience of alienation, of alterity, was also the shared experience of blacks in the United States and colonized Others in territories as far-flung as French-occupied Martinique and Algeria.

Gilroy's analysis, like that of DuBois and Fanon before him, is a global argument which applies to all blacks whether in the Caribbean, the wider Americas, or Europe. Thus the problem of a prophetic future, the problem of what to do when faced with nihilist confrontations, with mechanisms of an a priori superiority, with structures of domination, leads, in my mind, not to a calcified or fossilized conception of self, but rather to a shared condition of exclusion as that experienced by blacks in the diaspora. Nevertheless, though the condition of members of the black diaspora is shared, it does not automatically follow that one solution to the problem of black identity will be adequate for all members of that diaspora. A facile answer to the problem of exclusion may compel the advocacy of a uniqueness, a distinctive, essentialist selfhood or group identity to which all such excluded are said to belong. Thus, the search for a Caribbean identity, for example, or any other kind of identity which falls prey to the essentialist pitfall will be a shortsighted solution at best.

In speaking too quickly and seriously of a Caribbean identity, we may be on the verge of exhibiting the very residual condition of which Gilroy warns us:

> The traditional teaching of ethics and politics—practical philosophy— came to an end some time ago, even if its death agonies were prolonged. This tradition had maintained the idea that a good life for the individual and the problem of the best social and political order for the collectivity could be discerned by rational means. Though it is seldom acknowledged even now, this tradition lost its exclusive claim to rationality partly through the way that slavery became internal to western civilisation and through the obvious complicity which both plantation slavery and colonial regimes revealed between rationality and the practice of racial terror. Not perceiving its residual condition, blacks in the west eavesdropped on and then took over a fundamental question from the intellectual obsessions of their enlightened rulers. Their progress from the status of slaves to the status of citizens led them to enquire into what the best possible forms of social and political existence might be.[12]

Here, Gilroy warns us, inter alia, of the tendency to conflate collective identity with the sociopolitical. Modes of liberal democratic governance, even if one were to acquiesce to thoughts of a political identity, do not seem to touch on the significant concerns disscussed here. Groups in the throes of repression, of domination, of creolization are often creative groups. One does not tell a creative person when and how to be creative. The time and manner of creativity are typically personal if not creative choices. This simple principle of individual freedom at the level of the creative ought to apply to groups as well.

Composite Identities

The problem presented by the Caribbean is that it is a novel condition requiring a novel response. In the Caribbean region, there has been a tendency to swallow "head and tail" the belief that liberal democracies and their entourage would solve the problem exemplified by the Caribbean condition. The Caribbean condition, as articulated within Gilroy's motif of the ship, is one of relation. It consists in the relationship of a multitude of cultures and persons in transition. It is arguably the condition of diasporic peoples. Can an identity be assigned to such a people, to such a condition, to such a territory and place? What can the Caribbean suggest regarding issues of governance and control consequent upon the nature of the region's historical uprooting of peoples? Are we forever condemned to see the past in the present, or are we better placed to avoid a nihilistic future following on the analyses of Trouillot, West, Carby, and Gilroy? Edouard Glissant does not provide us with immediate answers to the questions proposed above. However, he articulates several principles of the condition of identity in the Caribbean. He is silent on the notion that Caribbean identity is a political formation, silent on the notion as represented by the OAS, for example, that Caribbean identity is to be discovered in some burgeoning liberal democratic space. I have suggested above, as in the discussion of Haiti, that this form of political identity is lacking in the context of a viable Caribbean identity formation. Such a notion would rely on an individual ontology, whereas the Caribbean environment and experience speaks more properly to a social ontology, an ontology of relations.

Glissant, like Gilroy, makes use of a particular conception of space to explain the presence and influence of people of African descent, as well as others, in the contemporary Caribbean context. He suggests that:

Les Africains traités dans les Amériques portèrent avec eux par-delà les Eaux Immenses la trace de leurs dieux, de leurs coûtumes, de leurs langages. Confrontés au désordre implacable du colon, ils connurent ce génie, noué aux souffrances qu'ils endurérent, de fertiliser ces traces, créant, mieux que des synthèses, des résultantes dont ils eurent le secret. Les langues créoles sont des traces frayées dans la baille de la Caraïbe et de l'océan Indien.[13]

[Africans trafficked in the Americas brought with them over the Immense Waters the trace of their gods, their customs, their languages. Confronting the colonizer's implacable disorder, they possessed the genius, tied to the sufferings they endured, to cultivate these traces, creating, better than syntheses, results for which they alone had the secret. The Creole languages are traces carved out of the Caribbean sea and the Indian ocean.][13]

We have in Glissant's words the Caribbean as an example of a "chaos-monde" where cultures clash, attract, and become intimate with each other. The "chaos-world," in effect, is the state of the world in our day. It is a temporal state of affairs that exhibits the complex relationships of cultures. We live more rapidly and more immediately than before the advent of electronic technology. The novelty of the Caribbean is that it provides us, because of its diversity of peoples and cultures, a space of study, a laboratory of identity whereby the interactions of cultures can be examined as lived.

Glissant, like Gilroy, speaks of "ship-spaces" as spaces of development for creole societies. The New World is such a space. The very temporality of this "chaos-world" negates the viability of fixed identity. However, to deny that there is any fixed identity is not to disregard an assessment of the conditions under which contemporary Caribbean peoples live. The condition of poverty or misery in Haiti, for example, cannot be dismissed or disconnected from the nation's historical links with other countries which have participated in exclusionary practices. At the same time, however, Glissant's analysis speaks compellingly of the need to avoid the limitedness of fixed categories of identity rooted in such historical relations.

A Provisional Conclusion

As a corollary to Glissant's assessment that creolization is more representative of postmodern movements of peoples and minds, and Gilroy's argument that the black Atlantic impregnated the industrial and technological strength of the West, the concept of a transitional identity, perhaps implicit in the phrase *diasporic identity*, is an appropriate representation of the activities of collectivities such as are found in the Caribbean context. Transitional identity rejects the stasis of the aforementioned limited conceptions of identity in order to promote the idea of identity, say, Caribbean identity as more properly a process, a kind of kinetic activity. The foregoing discussion has suggested, through its search for possible locations of Caribbean identity, that first one is Caribbean by force. One is Caribbean because one is at the margin. The thought of alterity is particularly well expressed in the work of Gilroy and Glissant as they are represented here. Gilroy's use of the "ship" as the laboratory where the New World emerges is complemented by Glissant's observation that the relations exhibited in the Caribbean speak to the future of a New World culture of conviviality.

It might be suggested that one is Caribbean for having accepted, for the most part unequivocally, the dogma of political homogeneity and economic unification. It can be argued that the Caribbean, as it has adopted the prevailing economic and political trends, has accepted its marginalization and has not critically considered, at the level of identity concerns, whether the calls for democratization are universally applicable. Such acquiescence at the level of identity formation is quite probably the result of a lingering postcolonial attitude that encourages a blind following in the footsteps of the more successful members of the global political and economic environment. Underlying the ready adoption of such approaches is a belief, in my view, that these exemplars of success owe their international position to the presumed strength of these all too readily accepted principles of development and governance.

Notes

1. See Cornel West, "Philosophy, Politics and Power: An Afro-American Perspective," *Philosophy Born of Struggle*, ed. Leonard Harris (Dubuque, Iowa: Kendall/Hunt, 1983), 51. Hereafter 'PPP," cited in the text.

2. The complete list of countries can be found in the "Colombian Tourist Visa Requirements" published by the "Consulado Generál de Colombia" in Chicago. The list used for the purposes of this essay was dated 11 April 1997.

3. Domingo Acevedo, "The Haitian Crisis and the OAS Response: A Test of Effectiveness in Protecting Democracy," *Enforcing Restraint*, ed. Lori Fisler Damrosh (New York: Council on Foreign Relations Press, 1993), 115.

4. Ibid., 123.

5. Michel Rolph Trouillot, *Silencing the Past* (Boston: Beacon Press, 1995).

6. See, for example, Robert A. Dahl, *Who Governs?* (New Haven, Conn.: Yale University Press, 1961).

7. Robert A. Dahl, *Dilemmas of Pluralist Democracy* (New Haven, Conn.: Yale University Press, 1982), 4.

8. See Hazel Carby, *Reconstructing Womanhood* (Oxford: Oxford University Press, 1987). Hereafter *RW*, cited in the text.

9. See Carby's assessment of Barbara Welters's notion of "true womanhood" in *Reconstructing Womanhood*, 23.

10. Paul Gilroy, *The Black Atlantic* (Cambridge: Harvard University Press, 1993), 16.

11. See, for example, Iris Young, *Justice and the Politics of Difference* (Princeton, N.J.: Princeton University Press, 1990), chap. 5.

12. Gilroy, *Black Atlantic*, 39.

13. Edouard Glissant, *Introduction à une poétique du divers* (Paris: Gallimard, 1996), 70–71.

Mirage in the Mirror: Album Cover Imagery in Caribbean Music

Mike Alleyne

Middle Tennessee State University

T HIS essay explores aspects of the relationship between the visual media used to sell Caribbean music and the music itself and some of the broad cultural implications and potentialities resultantly arising. Although this is written with specific reference to the Anglophone Caribbean, the complexities highlighted here are arguably equally relevant to artists in other regional territories. The psychological construction of the Caribbean is perhaps most tellingly achieved through the use of visual images to which the region's music provides an accompanying soundtrack. This mode of representation may, however, present distorted or stereotypical images filtered through ideologically obscured lenses. Thus, questions are raised regarding the extent to which such modes provide accurate reflection of Caribbean cultural and artistic identity and expression. Through assessment of the ongoing interconnectivity between the music and the visual representations used to achieve its marketability, it is possible to reach some general conclusions about the state of both internal and external cultural perceptions of the Caribbean.

The ultimate validity (or invalidity) of possible meanings produced through textual engagement is determined by the consumer, but only within the framework of the limited variety of visual texts to which the consumer is exposed. Particularly relevant here is the critical proposition that "which codes are mobilized will largely depend on the triple context of the location of the text, the historical moment and the cultural formation of the reader."[1] While this subject presents varied possibilities for clinical application of structuralist and poststructuralist theory, strict superimposition of such critical principles is best avoided since, among other factors, assessment of the character of Caribbean music's visual representation is still in relative infancy (as is definition of many of the relevant cultural parameters).

With the advent of the music video as a principal marketing tool in the early 1980s, the significance of visual representation in Caribbean music was firmly established and heightened. Without the exploitation of this visual opportunity the relative commercial success of those artists exhibiting various degrees of Caribbean identity would have been far more difficult to attain. The mainstream (and notably ephemeral) presence of Shabba Ranks, Maxi Priest, or Ini Kamoze is as much due to the assertion of visual identity afforded by major label backing and dissemination as it is to their suitably configured "crossover breakthrough" material. However, both the application of video and its crucial marketing component, the album cover, have exhibited signs of a more widespread phenomenon: "a shrinking repertoire of visual signs."[2]

Where music video is concerned this usually involves combining liberal displays of flesh, clichéd dance routines, and manufactured visual narratives. Moreover, this limitation of scope manifests itself strongly within the music as aural formulas and stereotypes make performers progressively less individually distinguishable, ever more frequently due to unimaginative applications of digital music technology in an age dominated by machine culture. Both visual modes—the music video and the album cover—provide insight into the types of patterns of self/other perception and representation that have assumed ideological dominance and, to some extent, the cultural mechanics of their construction and development. We may literally "read" the texts for indications of the past, present, and perceived future of the artist as rendered both by the performer and the other creative determinants—art/video director and record company.

While video has perhaps become the more obvious topic for textual analysis due to its broadly acknowledged power in influencing market taste, its comparatively ancient predecessor, the album cover, begs for closer consideration. The dominance of music video is by no means disconnected from album-cover art since it has heavily influenced those representations of artistic identity in recent years by virtually demanding coordination between the two modes.[3] This essay attempts a partial deconstruction of the album cover text to discuss a few of the important aspects of the narratives encoded therein and to suggest where larger discourses may be at work.

Brief Historical Background

The role of the album cover in Caribbean music is, in some ways, quite enigmatic. Despite the decades of its use which have provided the potential for its maturation as a useful visual signpost and complement to aural content, a limited range of dominant images have instead been consistently reiterated in a manner implying cultural stasis. This examination assumes that the pervasive literal visual narrative is often insufficient to convey the complexity of Caribbean artistic and historical experience inherent in the musical texts. Thus, it is useful to consider the relationship of the visual representations to the musical manifestations, and in particular whether the album cover has functioned as a reinforcement and validation of cultural distinctiveness or as a confirmation of an outdated valuation of both the music and culture. Are the images accurately representative of the Caribbean as a clear reflection of a recognizable self and/or community? Is there instead a refracted, distorted visage which has no sufficiently meaningful cultural point of reference within this phase of the region's history? In many ways, attaining the answers to these and other questions relates directly to the simultaneous intangibility and apparent concreteness of a reflected image which can be readily perceived by the senses, yet never fully retrieved. As with a reflection, a clear presence is evident, yet ultimately elusive and transient.

In much the same way that repetitive, mechanical use of digital technology has made Caribbean music vulnerable to criticisms of excessive commercialization, the underexploited potential of its visual dimensions similarly reflects what might be described as "technocide." This is self-inflicted cultural injury through an inadequate use of technology, whereby it imprisons or fixes instead of liberating via fulfillment of its potential. The dominant cover images contribute to a media-propelled construction in which the many dimensions comprising the Caribbean experience are probably misrepresented and consumed, both in the sense of commercial transaction and of ontological engulfment. The representations appear primarily limited by basic marketing considerations based on the necessity of evoking canonized imagery of the Caribbean in the consumer's mind.

The Significance of Album Covers

The misleading idea that the album cover is merely a transparent luxury with little active relationship to the music it envelops should immediately be dispelled (despite the unfortunate existence of numerous examples fostering this illusion). Not only does the design of an album cover directly influence how we "see" the music, but the very terms in which musicians describe their works underscore audio-visual interpenetration. As Andrew Goodwin notes, "references to colors, tone, shades, space, and the musical 'palette' are common ways of thinking among the producers of popular music."[4] Thus, appropriate value is ascribed to the inherent textual significance of the cover, and not only within a pictorial context but also inclusive of "the symbolic implications of typeface and tones."[5] Despite a general tendency to discard the significance of such ancillary pictorial elements as incidental devices, we must recognize that the printed representations of an album title or artist's name shapes our perception of the music in one way or another.[6]

Gilroy suggests that "the cultural significance of record covers as a form of folk art is . . . enhanced simply because they offer one of very few opportunities to see and enjoy images of black people outside the stereotyped guises in which the dominant culture normally sanctions their presence."[7] This observation points toward the potential of the album cover as a truly meaningful signifier of cultural and creative identity and indirectly invites consideration as to whether this potential is being realized in a variety of musical contexts, including those of the Caribbean. The inevitable reduction of cover size on the CD insert versus the vinyl album sleeve is a crucial issue. It provides both a symbolic indication of a confining reduction of artistic scope and options within the music industry's mainstream and an inversely disproportionate representation of the ever-growing dominance of visual media as gateways to aural art.

From Peter Kemper's perspectives of artistic aesthetics and sensory impact, "the small CD format with its antiseptic, plastic 'jewel box' feel restricts the play of surface textures, of cardboard, and paper, the tactile stimulus, the printing intensity, the washes and coatings . . . precludes the possibility of immersing oneself in an image."[8] Although Kemper's point is not uniformly true—since this very essay is largely based on immersion within the images of even CD art—he is accurate in highlighting the limited possibilities for such immersion given the limited physical dimensions of the CD. Ideally, the cover makes a statement through which it affirms that the musical contents are consistent or in conflict with our expectations or preconceptions.

This coded visual narrative imbued with subliminal nuance is a sensory appetizer foreshadowing the flavor of the hopefully sumptuous main course. If, however, this appetizer lacks appeal or is unsatisfying in some important facet, then little incentive exists to explore further by delving into the musical artistic substance. If our sense of adventure remains unchallenged by this visual medium and clichés pass for individual statements, then the very medium is in dire danger of invalidity. Implicit here is the logical assumption that the cover functions directly as an appropriate advertisement for the musical content since representation on other bases disconnects the amorphous relationship between text and visual manifestation. Thus, the cover may also represent the projection or assimilation of disjunctive cultural ideology.

Virtually parallel with the explosion of computer-related technology application in popular music and the artistic homogenization which has accompanied it, there has been a comparable lack of abstraction among the album covers. Understandably, the earlier calypso album covers of the 1950s and 1960s were limited in thematic scope largely due to the colonial hegemony which presented essentialized perceptions of black artistry. Moreover, a mere handful of recording companies dominated the business in this era, sharing the same culturally and commercially exploitative vision. The portrayal of stereotypes (which are still forcefully present) was perhaps at its strongest then—the smiling native in brightly colored clothing, captured in the midst of provocative gyration (or stimulating it amongst others)—the Caribbean seen through a colonizer's touristic prism of sea, sun, sand, and sex. The only vaguely redeeming factor here is that the older cover representations probably bear a loosely approximate relationship to the fundamental textual concerns and articulation of the music, despite the undeniable layers of lyrical ambiguity and musical ingenuity underscoring calypso craftsmanship.

In addition, where the early days of calypso, ska, and reggae are concerned, the frequent substitution of female flesh for an image of the artist, still amply demonstrated on Byron Lee's records in the present day, reinforced limitations on the scope of imagery through which the Caribbean could be effectively commercially represented. The limited availability of visual examples of these older Caribbean album covers implies that the medium has not been taken seriously as a cultural indicator. Specifically, there appear to be no retrospective collections of cover art imagery representing the region's music, whereas such compilations are integral in underlining the historical significance of other music forms in other cultures in the electronic age.

The apparent scarcity of abstraction—then and now—can in part be interpreted as a means of directly conveying the music's kinetic immediacy and concrete accessibility. Alternatively, this might also be seen as a failure to explore the deeper dimensions of the complex and historically tormented Caribbean psyche. The role of limited promotional funding is probably not a sufficiently significant factor in inhibiting the presentation of an imaginative or visually disarming concept, but is more likely relevant to the extent to which the idea can be effectively realized. The pervasive, mechanical visual reproduction of slight variations on a few limited themes cannot be explained away quite so easily. A more likely factor is the artist and/ or record company perception of the role of cover imagery as merely secondary to both the old and new audiences for this music. With rare, notable exceptions, the cover appears to be perceived as having little impact on the buyer's receptiveness, other than to confirm expectations of the musical narrative.

The literal cover may frequently intend to represent a stripping-away of superfluous adornment, presenting the raw, natural self or community. In this way, even the repetition of basic images seems wholly appropriate to the music contained therein. However, the implications for asserting distinctive creative identity—vital to the growth of any art form—are far less positive. The visual homogeneity is a clear, unfortunate complement to representations of Caribbean music within which the relationship between foreground and background elements are locked in formulaic stasis.

Jamaican Popular Music

In reggae culture, a few modes of visual formulas are especially dominant. Most commonplace is the use of portraiture, especially the close-range photo headshot of the artist, in smiling, aggressive, or pensive mood, or in the act of performance. This type of forthright presentation of the artist is often accompanied by a stereotypically tropical background. Depictions of the female body in photos and illustrations are frequently used, especially on compilations of various artists, to relate inherent danceability and erotic sensuality. Illustrations utilizing red, green, and gold, especially in flag form, signifying consciousness and acceptance of African heritage, are also pervasive. Few examples exist of efforts to transcend these fundamental formats.

Interestingly though, the cover art on dub[9] releases frequently provides clear evidence of diversion from formula. Certainly, the aural abstraction of the genre calls for an appropriate visual complement perhaps more than any other form of Caribbean music. The cover of the U.K.-based Revolutionary Dub Warriors album *State of Evolution* (On U Sound, 1996) presents a striking image in which the

leaves of a marijuana plant in the foreground are tellingly juxtaposed against the instantly recognizable Babylonian symbol of London's Big Ben, all set against an ominous, apocalyptic backdrop that
echoes the texture of the music itself. Here, the subversion of the
status quo is both imminent and explicit, and the illustration's
depth of field is adequately demonstrative of dub's depth of tone,
color, and dimension.

In addition to addressing the cover art of dub releases, it is also
instructive to examine their visual relationship to their formal predecessors—the art for the release upon which the dub sequel is
based (where this is the case). The *Space and Time* CD (Ras, 1995) by
Mystic Revealers is typically literal, presenting a conventional band
photo superimposed on an illustration of a planetary sphere, with
symbols of time merging in the background. With its dub counter-
part, *Space and Dub* (Ras, 1996), group members are missing altogether—a regular feature of cover art in the dub genre—perhaps
visually reflecting the musical shift from straightforward textual
reading. There is still the very literal representation of time, but in
this instance the dominant image of a comprehensively shattered
clock face perfectly captures the suspension, fragmentation, and disintegration of both time and space within dub, generally, and specifically on this album. Thus, the dub CD cover here, perhaps paradoxically, provides a more creatively complementary visual
statement, with both literal *and* abstract representations of the musical texts.

Reggae Artists' Logos

The use of logos acting in effect as an artist's visual trademark
from album to album is a strategy seldom employed in reggae culture (and is, therefore, only briefly assessed here). This approach is
sometimes seen as a manifestation of corporate assimilation within
the music industry and, perhaps in consequence, it has been either
resisted or ignored by many performers despite its visual artistic util-
ity in consolidating individual identity. In many cases (outside of
reggae), the logo has contributed to the creation of visual narrative
continuity from one release to the next. Two comparatively rare instances of logo usage in Caribbean music are provided by the groups
Steel Pulse and Third World.

One might point to the series of major label ties in the history of
Steel Pulse and the progressive homogenization of the group's
music as underlying factors which their logo gradually came to sym-

bolize: creative stasis within the political economy of the corporate music industry. The recognizability of their visual identity ran counter to the growing inability of the group's core audience to identify with the excessively commercially transformed material or, moreover, to associate this with the perceived cultural and ideological authenticity which the logo had implicitly represented. Third World also carried its own distinctive logo on its earliest albums (from 1976 to 1981) with complementary artwork creating an aura of cultural authenticity rather than commercial incorporation.

Significantly, their shift from Island Records to Columbia (now Sony) produced increased commercialization of their music and was significantly accompanied by their logo being jettisoned. Similarly, the group's subsequent tenure with Polygram (now part of the megalithic Universal Records empire) indicated a virtually parallel erosion of visual and musical identities, with an unabashed emphasis on commercial material lacking the creative substance of the earlier works which had established their identity in the first instance. Evidently, then, as the material became more directly focused at a mainstream audience, their visual identity was similarly transformed to become less distinctive.

The Portrayal of Women

The representations of women have usually exploited sexual stereotypes, providing ample fuel for feminist critique. However, in recent times far more images have emerged of the female figure as dominant or empowered in this context. The cover of *Scent of Attraction* (Epic, 1995) by dancehall queen, Patra, offers at least two levels of visual exposure. What the consumer is shown on the cover is the black and white photo of Patra with a self-assured expression and lips starkly accented in red emphasizing the sensual core of her confidence. When the insert is unfolded a more complete picture emerges of the dancehall protagonist as the object of both potent lust and quasi-divine adoration, thus fulfilling the power narrative of sexual desirability and self-determination iterated in her musical texts. This is not to suggest that such portrayal is unambiguous, since ironically it is at least potentially self-subversive; it asserts female power only within a very limited visceral, carnal context, thereby perhaps undermining construction of a female totality inclusive of a complex psychological depth. Furthermore, it might well be argued that the appearance of seemingly more progressive visual representation is merely opportunistic recommodification of the female body relatively compatible with present ideological currents. This aspect of album cover representation probably requires an entirely separate discussion, inclusive of a comprehensive sociohistorical analysis perhaps as yet unapplied to this dimension of popular culture.

Calypso/Soca: The Case of Ice Records

Eddy Grant's Ice Records provides us with a rare case of movement toward visual abstraction on calypso album covers. Interestingly, this is an abstraction within which the physical representation of the artist has virtually vanished. The implications here need not be completely negative in view of the history of excessive, clichéd presentations of performers on their album covers within this genre. The visual style frequently departs from photographic portraiture altogether, instead utilizing illustrations which more suggestively symbolically convey the elemental content of the music. The material is thus infused with a sense of imagination and creative scope and possibilities in the minds of many consumers.

The international marketing focus of Ice, and its position as the premier outlet for calypso in major foreign markets has apparently led the label to carefully assess the imagery it utilizes in selling its merchandise. Its uncommon approach has created both a cohesive label identity through its cover designs and an assertion of the creative imagination and potential inherent within Caribbean music. The visual text of each release calls upon the consumer to read meaning into it rather than to receive a literal narrative requiring little or no subsequent consideration. The album covers do not employ readily recognizable symbols of calypso culture and thus transcend reinforcement of negative consumer conditioning. Theoretically, this long-overdue re-vision of the calypso album cover complements the label's attempts at musical stylistic innovation via the "ringbang" phenomenon. Given its almost inextricable relationship to calypso culture and consumer markets, the extent of its aural innovation is still a debatable point. Nonetheless, the strategies of Ice point to the critical need for textual unification, a cohesiveness of identity between aural and visual representation in a form which highlights fresh creative potentialities versus reiteration of largely redundant visual statements.

Conclusion

The clear proposition here is that the visual aspect of textual identity of Caribbean album covers displays (often inadvertently) a direct relationship to shifts in cultural and artistic representation. The evidence suggests the presence of a negative interrelationship between the recurrent visual texts and the musical texts which they purport to represent, and it appears that a considerably broader vision must emerge (both internally and externally) to encompass imaginative intangibilities as well as material realities. Much more work needs to be conducted in this area to uncover the cultural narratives revealing psychological and sociological perspectives on the Caribbean and its musical art. This is particularly important since there are few media so readily available and so extensively transmitted which have the potential to provide poignant reflections if we are prepared to examine the actual image, not merely the mirage.

Notes

1. John Storey, *An Introductory Guide to Cultural Theory and Popular Culture* (Athens, Ga.: University of Georgia Press, 1993), 80.

2. Jody Berland, "Sound, Image and Social Space: Music Video and Media Reconstruction," *Sound & Vision: The Music Video Reader*, ed. Simon Frith, Andrew Goodwin, and Lawrence Grossberg (London: Routledge, 1993), 30.

3. Paul Gilroy, "Wearing your art on your sleeve: Notes towards a diaspora history of black ephemera," *Small Acts: Thoughts on the Politics of Black Cultures* (London: Serpent's Tail, 1993), 255.

4. Andrew Goodwin, *Dancing in the Distraction Factory: Music Television and Popular Culture* (Minneapolis: University of Minnesota Press, 1992), 51.

5. See Felix Cromey, "A New Perspective: Sleeve Notes for Reid Miles," *Blue Note: The Album Cover Art*, ed. Graham Marsh, Felix Cromey, and Glyn Callingham (San Francisco, Calif.: Chronicle, 1991), 7.

6. Steve Lake, "Looking at the Cover," *ECM—Sleeves of Desire: A Cover Story* (Baden: Lars Muller, 1996), 257.

7. Gilroy, "Wearing your art on your sleeve," 243.

8. Peter Kemper, "Along the Margins of Murmuring," *ECM—Sleeves of Desire*, 10, 11.

9. The use of this term here refers only to the sonically spatial textual deconstruction of reggae's core elements which emerged from Jamaican studios in the early 1970s. It is necessary to make this distinction since in some Caribbean territories in recent years the term *dub* has been (mis)applied almost exclusively to Jamaican dancehall.

The Project of Becoming for Marlene Nourbese-Philip and Erna Brodber

Patricia Saunders

Bowdoin College

> Speech, voice, language, and word—all are ways of being in the world, and the artist working with the I-mage and giving voice to it is being in the world. The only way the African artist could be in this world, that is the New World, was to give voice to this split I-mage of voiced silence. Ways to transcend that contradiction had to and still have to be developed, for that silence continues to shroud the experience, the I-mage and so the word.
> —Marlene Nourbese-Philip, "The Absence of Language or How I Almost Became a Spy"

THE epigraph above captures what Lizabeth Paravasini and Barbara Webb refer to as the incomplete sense of history that is a central part of contemporary Caribbean women's writing for a number of reasons. Representing a broad spectrum of writing in the archipelago, "On the Threshold of Becoming: Caribbean Women Writers" discusses the works of writers from English-, French-, and Spanish-speaking countries. In their discussion of narratives written by Caribbean women writers between 1968 and 1984, Paravasini and Webb engage an array of texts which include Zee Edgell's *Beka Lamb*, Merle Hodge's *Crick Crack Monkey*, Michelle Cliff's *Abeng*, Paule Marshall's *The Chosen Place, The Timeless People*, and Jean Rhys's *Wide Sargasso Sea*. Their assertion is that the lack of closure in these novels is indicative of protagonists whose lives are "poised on the threshold of becoming." Their essay is central to my understanding of the recent body of work by Caribbean women writers. "On the Threshold of Becoming" examines contemporary critical perspectives on Caribbean women's writing, both to lay claim to a tradition already well established in important ways and to point to the shortcomings of critical interpretative tools for reading this body of work. According to Paravasini and Webb, the prevailing perspective in some feminist

133

criticism that writings by Caribbean women should "shed male-centered views and stress female determination" while showing women "in the process of emancipation from patriarchal institutions and values" has been an obstacle preventing useful critical interpretations of Caribbean women's writing.[1]

Paravisini and Webb's approach assumes that "patriarchal institutions" are easily distinguishable and do not implicitly already contain paradigms of "female self-determination." Their approach does not question the categories of history and identity, but seeks a feminist context for them. Whether we can define critical issues as "patriarchal" depends largely upon the agendas at work in constructing and interpreting postcolonial literature. However, the two categories/institutions of history and identity, while providing a central point of engagement for Caribbean writers, have also progressively been deployed effectively to decenter women's experiences in favor of a more nationalist perspective. In such a context, the nation signifies male struggle, authority, and sovereignty. This is so despite the continued narrative representations of the nation as overtly gendered (female) and specifically sexualized through the mapping of nationalist agendas onto women's bodies.

In the last ten years, there has been a dramatic increase in texts written by women in the Caribbean. Not only have women writers begun to produce more literary texts, but their works are widely read by audiences across the Caribbean, the United States, Canada, Africa, and Europe. A body of critical literature about Caribbean women's writing is also emerging, launched by Carole Boyce Davies and Elaine Savory Fido's volume, *Out of the Kumbla* (1990), Selwyn Cudjoe's anthology, *Caribbean Women Writers* (1990), and Evelyn O'Callaghan's *Woman Version* (1993). This body of critical writing pays particular attention to Caribbean women's narratives and what they bring to bear on contemporary debates about negotiating and narrating identity, difference, and culture in a national(ist) context.

The phrase "Caribbean women's writing" is not meant to suggest a uniformity about contemporary women's writing. Moreover, this phrase is not meant to suggest that women writers have only recently begun writing in the Caribbean, although it is the contemporary juncture that I will focus on in this essay.[2] Engaging the tropes of Caribbean literature, women writers have written about slavery, colonialism, and all of the complexities of colonial societies in the context of race, class, language, migration, exile, and postindependence struggles. My use of the phrase "Caribbean women's writing" is directed more at a school of thought that has emerged in recent writing produced by women in the archipelago, one that is distinct in its approach and understanding of being and identity in Caribbean literature.

One of the important distinctions most often made between Caribbean women's writing and that of their male counterparts is their varying perspectives on the experience and implications of colonialism. The recent emergence of Caribbean women's writing needs to be considered in the broader context of the rise of nationalist literatures and of the interests in nationalist struggles around the world. The recent crises of nationalist movements around the globe has led to an increased necessity for new ways of understanding both the phenomenon itself and its variations, claims, shortcomings. One of the most challenging factors facing several nationalist movements is the liberties taken in the name of "community." Benedict Anderson's definition of the nation as an "imagined community" marks the fundamental similarities between the role and importance of imagination in conceptualizing the bonds that draw a nation together. The recent increase, however, in waves of ethnic cleansing, break-away states, coup attempts, and the continued civil rights violations in the United States and other "superpowers" all point to the extent to which the role of the imagination as a force for instituting societies needs to be examined in a more critical context.

The crucial importance of such a consideration arises not simply out of the need for something "new" but from the emergence of sociohistorical circumstances which demand more expansive interpretations. The possibilities which lie within these new forms of knowing, as Cornelius Castoriadis argues in *The Imaginary Institution of Society,* need to be explored as realistic alternatives to inherited ways of thinking and knowing. In an effort to engage the problematic of the question of society and of history, Castoriadis suggests that the two need to be taken into consideration as one and the same: that is to say, the question of the social-historical. According to Castoriadis:

> Inherited ways of thinking can make only fragmentary contributions to this elucidation [of the question of society and that of history]. Perhaps this contribution is mostly negative, marking out the limits of a mode of thought and exposing its impossibilities . . . On the one hand, the inherited way of thinking has never been able to separate out the true object of this question and to consider it for itself. This object has almost always been split into a society, related to something other than itself and, generally, to a norm, end or *telos* grounded in something else, and a history, considered as something that happens to this society, as a disturbance in

relation to a given norm or as an organic or dialectical development towards this norm or *telos*. In this way the object in question, the being proper to the social-historical, is constantly shifted towards something other than itself and absorbed in it.[3]

The problematic outlined here is of singular importance for my discussion of Caribbean women's writing for a number of reasons. First, and most importantly, the centrality of Caribbean women's writing at this historical moment is indicative of an epistemological crisis. The crisis, as described by Castoriadis, rests in the stranglehold inherited thinking and modes of knowing have on our ability and desire to venture into untested waters, to experiment with alternative means of knowing and coming into knowledge.

It is no small coincidence that Caribbean women's writing has taken center stage during the current debates around the crises of nationalist struggles, particularly since their writing has served to highlight the insufficiency of current interpretative models to represent the complexities at work in this arena. As Marlene Nourbese-Philip suggests in her essay "The Absence of Writing or How I Almost Became a Spy," the project of self-possession and legitimization has shifted to grounds heretofore unmentioned, unheard, silenced: new imaginings. Several women writers have engaged the ideological and political silences in nationalist movements with respect to questions of ethnicity, gender, and class. Their representations of these critical questions highlight the contradictory nature of claims made in the name of the nation and its subjects. Novels such as Janice Shineborne's *The Last English Plantation*, Merle Collins's *Angel*, and Erna Brodber's *Louisiana* attempt to deform traditional nationalist discourses on history and identity by reimagining the very construction of these categories and the possibilities of alter/native modes of being. These alter/native modes of being include sociohistorical consciousness that emerges from nontraditional systems of knowledge production, psychic experiences, cultural and epistemological translations, and transmigrations.

As the ethnic conflicts represented in cultural productions and on political platforms in countries such as Trinidad, Jamaica, and Grenada suggest, the idea of a nation, imagined or otherwise, is not only difficult to sustain but may be quite perplexing if one considers the rapidity of migration and exchange (of people, discourses, currency, cultures) throughout the Caribbean. Moreover, the positioning of women in this imagined space is precarious and arguably functions to distract our attention from the ways in which the historical absence of women raises questions about the agendas at work in nation-building in its traditional configurations. The earlier limitations citizens faced with regard to migration opportunities and the possibilities of involvement in educational and governmental institutions have shifted and new opportunities have been opened. However, these new jobs and the greater availability of education for the broader population produced a new sense of urgency among colonial subjects about the ability of the "nation" to meet the needs of different segments of its communities.

Despite the apparent impossibility of nationalist projects, not just in the Caribbean but globally, new national movements are emerging daily, as sentiments about the need for autonomy within the state increase. I therefore want to examine the extent to which the recent body of Caribbean writing by women has begun to address the challenge of representing these movements and the difference they are concerned with preserving. My focus on women's writing from the Caribbean stems from my thinking about the ways national projects always already assume the second-class status of women within them. Regardless of the centrality of women to movements such as the Algerian Liberation Movement, the labor movements in Trinidad and Tobago, the civil rights movement in the United States, and so on, the extent to which any of these movements takes women's rights as part of its main goal and objective is minimal at best.

The recent critical emphasis on the plurality of various "imagined communities" has prompted several critics to adopt a more cross-cultural approach to examining cultural productions which define and are defined as "national" forms of expression. This attempt has meant a radical revision in both the cultural and critical interpretative tools we use to engage these productions. In one of the most recent critical texts dedicated solely to West Indian women's writing, *Woman Version: Critical Approaches to West Indian Fiction by Women,* Evelyn O'Callaghan describes the need to create new interpretative tools for reading this new body of writing. Drawing upon African American blues traditions, West Indian musical forms such as dub, and a long tradition of master narratives in Caribbean literature, O'Callaghan argues that the new body of West Indian women's writing is concerned with reproducing, remixing, writing over and thus creating its own versions of historical narratives which have typically constructed women as silent/absent subject. O'Callaghan suggests that a useful approach would be to:

> approach this writing, in light of the above, as a kind of remix or dub version, which utilizes elements from the "master tape" of Caribbean

literary discourse (combining, stretching, modifying them in new ways),
announces a gendered perspective, adds individual styles of "talk over,"
enhances or omits tracks depending on desired effect, and generally al-
ters by recontextualization to create a *unique* literary entity.[4]

O'Callaghan's observations here are similar to the set of concerns I
address in this essay. That is, her formulation of the "dub version"
in West Indian women's writing attempts to foreground a set of con-
tinuities, thematic concerns, and stylistic features in this body of literature.

Woman Version outlines a historical trajectory of women's writing
in the Caribbean, including the works of Caribbean-born white Creole women writing during the nineteenth century. The dub version
is an important critical tool for understanding women's writing in
relationship to the larger body of writing in the archipelago. However, I want to extend this idea to examine contemporary writing by
West Indian women. This writing adopts a new critical perspective
in order to highlight the limitations of colonial discourses that
frame the "quest for identity" and the "quarrel with history," two
long-standing traditions in Caribbean literature. To this end, I
would suggest that rather than thinking of West Indian women's
writing in terms of remixing master narratives, we might consider
this new body of writing as dis-forming the discourses which have
instituted these narratives and bestowed them with "master" status.

The dub version assumes a capacity and limitation on the possibilities for transgressing the score (or in the case of the literature, the
master narrative). The possibilities for transgressing the "score" in
master narratives lie in deploying traditional instruments of narration in order to revise the systems within which these representations circulate. Though historical representations may indeed circulate in a finite system of interpretation, the frequencies of utterances
articulated from these sites are limitless because they depend largely
on the capacity of the subject to adjust its interpretation to accommodate the musical or literary text. For example, dub music relies
heavily on its untranslatability in a global market of listeners. The
task of the translator in this case is not simply to translate from one
language to another, but to recognize the doubling of the capacity
of language in various systems of interpretation. The "stretching,
combining, and modifying" that O'Callaghan refers to extends to
the language of representation, not just the discursive terrain. In
this context, it is not simply what gets said, but how it is said, interpellated, by whom and for what specific purposes. Several Caribbean
women writers have begun to translate and transgress the scores, the

master narratives, by asserting that an emphasis on the content of history limits critical interventions into the construction of this category, history, and the knowledge which constitutes it as a discipline.

Historically, Caribbean literature written by women has been marginalized both because of social, cultural, and economical inequities based on gender and, more specifically, because its discourses have not been counted among the institutionalized modes of knowing. The contributors to *Trinidad* and *The Beacon*, for example, while attempting to construct a national literary tradition in the Caribbean, donned the hand-me-downs of their colonial masters and educators. While these writers were indeed revising Shakespeare, they did so by depending largely on the sturdiness of the fabric implicit in colonialist discourses. That is to say, their revisions assumed the legitimacy of already institutionalized discourses of belonging, based on colonial traditions of discovery and conquest so central to British national identity and culture. Moreover, the unities of discourse, or narratives about regaining territorial or political power in the Americas and Europe, worked to produce an unquestioned coherence within imperialist discourses and effectively reduced all difference within these traditions to a recognizable *same*. The only possibility available within this paradigm of sameness is of recognition based on a reflection of those terms and conditions set forth by imperialism. In the case of the Calibanesque tradition, all exchanges are always already framed and authorized by the colonial encounter and are therefore fixed and limited to a reflection or defective copy of an originary narrative. The impact of these "gifts" is best remembered as the curse Caliban suffers, even in his attempts at acts of subversion.

The question of how women, writing a generation later, were supposed to fashion their responses to newly independent nations and a growing sense of neocolonialist aggression, needs to be considered in order to understand these new forms of cultural expression. While critics have noted the revolutionary possibilities implicit in Caliban's (and other national heroes) claim to the island and thus to his freedom through his mother, Sycorax, most Caribbean women writers chose not to return to Shakespeare's play to launch their engagements with the "quarrel with history."[5] One of the major changes that made the reconceptualizations of *The Tempest* necessary was the mass migration of artists from the Caribbean to Great Britain and the United States in the 1940s and 1950s. The advent of waves of colonials headed to the motherland (here figured as Britain and later the United States) meant that new relationships between colonials and their former masters were being forged.

These migrations (or the "brain drain" as it is commonly called) marked both an epistemological and geographical shift in debates about national identities in the Caribbean. The "pleasure of exile" was not one shared by many women (writers or otherwise) at this historical juncture. I have therefore chosen to revise the title of George Lamming's collection of essays, *The Pleasures of Exile,* in order to read what he terms the "pleasure" of exile as an instance of privilege extended to very few women of his generation.

Despite the geographical similarities in migration patterns between contemporary Caribbean women writers and their male counterparts (during the 1950s and 1960s), the cultural and political circumstances surrounding these waves of migration were significantly different. The migration of women writers in the 1980s and 1990s was not hailed with the same sense of national pride as the previous exodus of the "sons of the nation." Moreover, the institutional assurances (such as jobs with the BBC, teaching posts, free-lance reporting, etc.) which helped to sustain writers and artists such as C. L. R. James, Denis Williams, and others were not available for women migrating a generation later. The absence of these benefits represents a continuing shift in racial politics regarding immigrants from the black diaspora, as well as drastic changes in relations between Britain and its former colonies. No longer the benevolent provider, Britain's cultural perspectives had shifted to a focus on taking care of its "own" and preserving a sense of Britishness.[6]

My interest in raising these issues is two-fold. First, my main focus is on the recent "boom" in Caribbean women's writing and the cultural and political conditions that necessitate shifts in theoretical and interpretative tools for reading and comprehending difference and national identity. Rather than reading this increase in the production and publication of Caribbean women's writing as proof positive that culture is yet another commodity in the maddening market of transnational capital, I want to argue that the increase in production, circulation, and dissemination of women's writing in the Caribbean diaspora is a concerted response to an epistemological crisis in our understanding of difference and identity. Second, I am interested in the ways in which narrative strategies work effectively to reconceptualize the subject of history and the ways in which the subject relates to and is related to its surroundings. Categories that have historically been understood as oppositional to the subject, such as history, narrative, identity and the self/other paradigm, are being reimagined and reconstructed in light of recent epistemological shifts in Caribbean literary traditions. Moreover, I am interested in the challenges these epistemological shifts pose to our understanding of ontology. That is to say, I want to examine the extent to which the "emergence" of Caribbean women's literature is intimately connected to the epistemological and ontological exigencies which necessarily attend changes in (inter)national identities and spaces.

Most important to my analysis in this essay is the idea of a political metaphysics, a metaphysics grounded in the necessity of creating *another* epistemic foundation for understanding being in a postmodern society. As such, my engagement with Nourbese-Philip's work is aimed at exploring the inextricable links between traditional constructions of nation and gender, as well as sexuality and the nature of being, links which reside in the silent spaces of the self. Although Nourbese-Philip's work demonstrates a different approach than that employed by Erna Brodber's writing (certainly where ontological questions are concerned), I am interested in the ways in which these two writers attempt to address the Caribbean's long-standing "quarrel with history."

Despite the absence of women's voices in the quarrel with history debates, contemporary writers are faced with new questions that present themselves in a slightly different context than that of their predecessors. While I would not assert that the writers I discuss here are concerned with the category of history in the same manner as earlier writers, I want to examine their emphasis on the category of history and the discursive formations that have historically comprised this category. The difference between these two approaches is that many of the writers engaged in the quarrel with history debates assume that the epistemic possibilities of history (as a category) are always already fixed, and that therefore no discussion of the knowledges which constitute the structural components of this field is deemed necessary. However, contemporary writers such as Nourbese-Philip are engaged in challenging the very category of history and the knowledges that enable such a category.

Where Nourbese-Philip and other writers like Dionne Brand and Merle Collins posit language and memory as the sites of engagement for wresting history away from the written word, Erna Brodber reaches beyond these paradigms to assert that the construction of knowing and being need to be reconsidered in a social-historical context. My examination of the work of Brodber and Nourbese-Philip is aimed at addressing several of the concerns mentioned above. These two writers bring new perspectives to current debates about history and identity in Caribbean literature. Though, as stated earlier, Nourbese-Philip's work is different from Brodber's in its critical and artistic interpretation of history and identity; her explicit linking of language, sexuality, and history in her poetry highlights the hegemony exercised by colonialist discourses. In this context, her thematic emphasis on language is similar to that of her male counterparts, but her critique of foreign language as a form of historical and sexual violence opens new frontiers that will inevitably have a significant impact on how we read post-neocolonial narratives.

Brodber's novel, *Louisiana*, suggests that memory is not the primary enabling force for the postmodern colonial subject. Rather, her representations of history rely largely upon imaginative spaces in the unconscious as a site of political and metaphysical intervention. Such a construction of history moves beyond the Calibanesque tradition and even beyond the dependence upon (written) language as the "true" signifier of historical presence. This construction opens critical spaces for engaging otherwise silenced spaces not as opportunities for "voicing" but as moments of translation between historical subjects and colonial subjects of history who have traditionally been characterized and understood as inaudible. The emphasis on translation for Brodber is in an effort to understand silence as a strategic positionality capable of signifying epistemological and ontological presence. The "silent spaces" of postcolonial, nationalist narratives, therefore, are shown to provide useful strategic narrative and political interventions into the ways we imagine and conceptualize national identities. Although these gaps effectively marginalized women historically, contemporary writers such as Brodber have transformed them into a space for mediating the complex transitions in nationalist projects, and this work has enhanced our ability to interpret these transitions.

One such shift contemporary Caribbean writing has brought to cultural and literary studies is a movement away from the oppositionality of theory and creative writing. For Caribbean writers, the two have never been, and could never be, mutually exclusive. For writers in the archipelago, the emergence of the Caribbean novel was simultaneously an achievement in imaginative art and a manifestation of critical reflection. Moreover, the nature of their existence demanded that these writers create themselves within the realm of the imaginary, and this act required a theoretical understanding of what was at stake in such a project. In this context, the work of contemporary Caribbean women writers is particularly significant because the stakes for them are much higher as a consequence of their long history of marginalization. The renewed effort to demolish the division between art and ideology speaks directly to the need for revising black nationalist discourses on identity and difference. Where early attempts at articulating oppositional discourses were con-

cerned with negotiation within the parameters established by hegemonic power structures, contemporary Caribbean women writers
have set out to dis-form these paradigms and the very realities they
are said to represent.

Nourbese-Philip's work examines the link between the violence of
foreign languages and the violence of sexual exploitation, bringing
both into proximity by means of an exploration of form and by an
examination of the discursive formations employed in racist practices. Brodber examines the politics of metaphysics in an effort to
privilege the areas of the unconscious that have been negated as viable sites of knowledge production. Brodber focuses on the imagination and other experiences of *physis*. The term *physis* is employed
here in the context of Martin Heidegger's definition in *An Introduction to Metaphysics*:

> *Physis* means the power that emerges and the enduring realm under its
> sway. This power of emerging and enduring includes "becoming" as
> well as "being" in the restricted sense of inert duration. *Physis* is the
> process of a-rising, of emerging from the hidden, whereby the hidden is
> first made to stand.[7]

This term, as I employ it in my reading of Brodber's narrative, is
meant to indicate a critical intervention similar to Edouard Glissant's notion of "opaqueness" whereby that which is hidden can be
made transparent through focusing on contradictions and obscurities. All of Brodber's narrative fiction is concerned with this opaqueness and the subject's ability to shed light on these obscurities. The
notion of *physis* as an experience similar to that of the imagination
is tied to the subject's manipulation of its surroundings such that
conceptualizing an-other set of possibilities is not only feasible, but
essential.

Thus, the category of history is no longer a site of dormancy but
an occasion for the growth of the subject's consciousness. This deployment of history as well as the breadth of what constitutes knowledge in history are two of the characteristics that distinguish contemporary Caribbean literature from the Trinidad Renaissance.
Nourbese-Philip's *She Tries Her Tongue, Her Silence Softly Breaks* is a particularly significant text in this regard. This collection engages the
theoretical and political implications of art and language in a post-
neocolonial historical context. Moreover, Nourbese-Philip launches
her critique of the politics of expression by resisting traditional constructions of both genre and gender in her works, marking the inter-
connectedness of theory/creative writing by questioning the binary

opposition traditionally constructed between them.[8] Nourbese-Philip's "Discourse on the Logic of Language" poses the problematic of language in a context which challenges the structured discourses and rules of poetry, form, and content.

Using prose, fiction, and poetry, Nourbese-Philip brings these otherwise distinct genres into the same space in order to examine the ways language, when employed and deployed in a particular way, imbues that which it expresses with meaning and power. Her poem, "Discourse on the Logic of Language," opens three times, in three different genres:

> English
> is my mother tongue.
> A mother tongue is not
> not a foreign lan lan lang
> language
> l/anguish
> anguish
> —a foreign anguish.   EDICT I

> English is   *Every owner of slaves*
> my father tongue   *shall, whenever*
>   *possible,*
> A father tongue is   *ensure that his slaves*
> a foreign language   *belong to as many*
> therefore English   *ethno-linguistic groups as*
> is a foreign language   *possible.*
> not a mother tongue
> not a mother tongue.   *If they cannot speak*
>   *to each other, they cannot*
>   *then foment rebellion*
>   *and revolution.*

> What is my mother
> tongue
> my mammy tongue
> my mummy tongue
> my momsy tongue
> my modder tongue
> my ma tongue?[9]

In what is definitely a poetic feat, Nourbese-Philip weaves several genres into her writing, placing them not only in dialogue with one another but visually and contextually on the same page in a historical and cultural context as well. These genre shifts force the reader to make important decisions in reading strategies, requiring the reader to give equal weight to all genres since they all appear in the same space, address the same theme, and thus need to be read in relation to one another.

By using gender to introduce the ways language communities are constructed, Nourbese-Philip draws the reader's attention to the exploitation embedded in the historical introduction of foreign languages in the New World. More specifically, by juxtaposing the ideology of mother and father tongues with EDICT I, the impact of singling out linguistic communities in order to prevent slaves in the New World from communicating, and therefore maintaining their native, or mother, tongues, stands as a testament to the ways in which language has been deployed in order to exploit and oppress. What is more, "Discourse on the Logic of Language" asserts historical and cultural links between language, sexuality, and oppression, as well as other links which manifest themselves in a variety of disciplinary discourses.

The act of writing which flows vertically up the left-hand margin of the page constructs an-other narrative, presumably fictive, that expresses the care administered by a mother to her child and the importance of the tongue as an object used to remove remnants of the afterbirth from the body of her newborn daughter. Though the writing is presented as a piece of fiction, a story narrated by an omniscient narrator, its relationship to the other texts on the page is significant because it is positioned in an authoritative relationship to the other discourses at work in the poem. Far from situating itself as fact or truth, the act of fiction is offered as a text which leans on the other discourses for its authority, depending on the reader's ability and willingness to connect it to the other representations on the page. The question of how fiction, as a genre, lends authoritative support to representations of society through its literal placement on the page is at the crux of Philip's critical project in this poem. However, as Castoriadis reminds us, imaginative productions are central for instituting what we think of as the real. In fact, these productions do more than just simply support the real, or what Castoriadis refers to as the "natural stratum":

The organization of this world leans on certain aspects of the first natural stratum, where it finds points of support, incitements, inductions. However, not only is it never purely and simply the repetition or reproduction of this stratum; it cannot even be described as a partial and selecting "sampling" of it. What is "sampled" is so only in relation to and on the basis of an organization of the world posited by society; it is so only by being *formed* and *transformed* in and through social institutions; and, finally but most importantly, this formation-transformation is *actual*, figured-presentified in and through modifications of the "sensible world": so that, finally, the very thing which is leaned on is *altered* by society by the very fact of this leaning on—which has strictly no equivalent in the physical world.[10]

In the passage above Castoriadis is describing the function of imaginative productions for instituting being within society. While the project of instituting being is not the primary concern of Nourbese-Philip in this collection, her critique of language and oppression speaks directly to the ways in which language and its deployment provide the foundations for interpreting and instituting modes of being.

Once more, Nourbese-Philip is very concerned with deconstructing the sensible in terms of social-historical institutions through a closer examination of the processes by which this sense is produced and disseminated, at times through coercion, terror, and legal and cultural practices and discourses. The marginal, capitalized narrative/discussion which occupies the same page as the poem and EDICT I is Nourbese-Philip's reconstruction of the locale of power and language in shaping identity. The story is of a child who, upon birth, is cleansed of what is presumably the residual film of the afterbirth. Here, the mother (tongue) is the progenitor of language and a source of protection:

WHEN IT WAS BORN, THE MOTHER HELD HER NEWBORN CHILD CLOSE: SHE BEGAN THEN TO LICK IT ALL OVER. THE CHILD WHIMPERED A LITTLE, BUT AS THE MOTHER'S TONGUE MOVED FASTER AND STRONGER OVER ITS BODY, IT GREW SILENT—THE MOTHER TURNING IT THIS WAY AND THAT UNDER HER TONGUE, UNTIL SHE HAD TONGUED IT CLEAN OF THE CREAMY WHITE SUBSTANCE COVERING ITS BODY. (*STHT*, 56)

In order to interpret this passage, one needs first to consider the multiplicity of meanings inherent in the telling of the story. That is to say, we cannot begin to understand this story without accepting that it is part of the dialectic created among the other texts on the page. As such, the different genres and discursive representations of the edict and the poem make two primary readings possible. One reading suggests that Philip's spatial arrangement of texts on the page provides a visual and discursive juxtaposing of the possible meanings. The mother tongue, in this instance, is the same organ described in the multiple-choice exam as an organ similar to the penis, sharing the description as a "tapering, blunt tipped, muscular, soft and fleshy organ" (*STHT*, 59). In this context, then, the actions of this mother have a different reading if we consider the duality implicit both in the actions and the language used to describe it. Tonguing, in this instance, becomes a verb in the sense of giving words. Therefore, rather than ensuring the reader of a definitive meaning or function, the options offered effectively dis-form the discourse by exposing the discursive terrain within which these historical definitions circulate.

At the same time, the implicit critique of the father tongue, or nation(al) language, which is said to be the voice of the larger community is not only challenged but dis-formed through Philip's engagement with the multiplicity of meaning in this poem. Once more, the scientific discourse, which appears on a page by itself, offers another complication in how we are to interpret this act of giving words. The distinction in this passage is of great significance for our understanding of the limitations of the apparently liberatory act of giving voice. The distinction between recognition of the spoken word and speaking the word highlights the contradictory nature of these acts once read through the historical lens that Philip provides in "Discourse on the Logic of Language." That is to say, although the mother's agency gives words to her daughter, it does not guarantee the context or conditions through which the daughter's utterances will be received or the field of play into which they will enter. The edicts, therefore, play an important role in enforcing the historical terror which produced a father tongue. The question of how women begin to articulate words (or try their tongues), which have been historicized into submission, is forcefully brought into the foreground in Philip's collection.

Nourbese-Philip's engagement with the discursive terrain of colonialist discourses effectively addresses another aspect of the "trying" nature of language and the politics of "trying tongues" which resist at every turn when their authority is put under a critical lens. Her emphasis on the historical manipulations of language for the purpose of oppression and exploitation highlights the systemic structures of nation languages, mother and father tongues, and the formation of linguistic and historical presence in history. Her critical examination of the phrase "mother tongue" privileges the constructing of the "mother" as the progenitor of language. The question Philip raises (of what we call a language that is a foreign language or foreign tongue) recognizes the implications of power which can circumvent the intimate act of tonguing and giving language to impose a foreign language.

EDICT II speaks directly to this question through the italicized emphasis placed on the proclamation that stresses the precise form of punishment exacted on slaves found communicating in their native tongues. Another edict appears later in "Discourse on the Logic of Language," one which considers a cure for any breach in the proclamation made in EDICT I:

> EDICT II
>
> Every slave caught speaking his native
> tongue shall be severely punished. Where
> necessary, removal of the tongue is
> recommended. The offending organ,
> when removed, should be hung on high in
> a central place, so that all passing may
> see and tremble.

> (*STHT*, 58)

The dilemma represented within and across these genres is examined further when we consider that among the historical practices of colonialism was the conscientious construction of communities which discouraged any means of intercommunity communication while at the same time implementing a language used to define labor and oppression. Within such a context, the mother tongue is tied intimately to the ideology of Africa and the New World, not simply as an originary space but as a space of empowerment.

But Nourbese-Philip does not limit her exploration of language to creative expression; she also explores scientific and educational discourses. Weaving the expressive language of all the various disciplines, she constructs one page of the poem as a multiple-choice exam. Focusing on the continued themes of language, mother tongue, slavery, and gender, Philip constructs an unusual but effective means of bringing the historical and political uses of these themes into dialogue with one another. Using the multiple-choice exam format, she enters into the discursive terrain of scientific language and examination:

> A tapering, blunt tipped, muscular, soft and fleshy organ describes
> (a) the penis.
> (b) the tongue.
> (c) neither of the above.
> (d) both of the above.
>
> In man, the tongue is
> (a) the principal organ of taste.
> (b) the principal organ of articulate speech.

    (c) the principal organ of oppression and exploitation.

The tongue
(a) is an interwoven bundle of striated muscle running in three planes.
(b) is fixed to the jawbones.
(c) has an outer covering of a mucous membrane covered with papillae.
(d) contains ten thousand taste buds, none of which is sensitive to the taste of foreign words.

Air forced out of the lungs up the throat to the larynx where it causes the vocal cords to vibrate and create sound. The metamorphic from sound to intelligible words requires
(a) the lip, tongue and jaw all working together.
(b) a mother tongue.
(c) the overseer's whip.
(d) all of the above or none.   (*STHT*, 59)

In addition to the unusual form Nourbese-Philip employs here, the thematics of the examination is particularly effective in the context of her critique of language, science, and oppression as it suggests the aim of mastery and skill. Each of the questions is skillfully crafted in order to highlight the similarities in the definitions and, most importantly, the implications of every possible selection. Once more, the inherent contradiction present in the possible selections highlights the extent to which the knowledge produced in various discourses depends largely upon the agendas at work in the dissemination of this knowledge. These contradictions are exemplified in the selections Nourbese-Philip's makes available to her readers. The final selection in the multiple-choice exam draws all of the choices in this question together to stress that the selections could be as equally true as false, depending on the agendas, perspectives, and positions of authority from which these decisions are made.

    By offering selections that are all correct answers to the question, the idea of choice in the poem becomes a precarious one. For example, the test-taker's decisions might depend largely upon the value of scientific knowledge or the discursive and historical connections between science and sociohistorical institutions. All decisions are, therefore, filtered through the authority of discursive communities which always already limit the possible selections from which we can choose. The scientific use of the tongue as an organ of taste, speech, expression, and exploitation is intimately tied to Nourbese-Philip's critique of gender oppression as it shares anatomical and physiological similarities with male genitals. Moreover, her engagement with scientific discourse brings our attention to the historical complicity between science, sexism, and racism.

Nourbese-Philip's project, then, is one of exposing the foundations of discursive uses of language and how they are deployed to construct the knowledge of certain objects, and even subjects, of history. In doing so, she exposes language and the knowledge produced from these vantage points as constructed and implicated in the hegemonic practices of linguistic and cultural oppression. The emphasis on knowledge and language in contemporary Caribbean women's writing reflects the significance of addressing the (L)aw of the land/nation which she describes as nine-tenths possession, and one-tenth legitimization. This is a significant refusal of institutionalized paradigms such as the Calibanesque tradition in that it departs from the usual historical emphasis on the "prison house of language" approach to colonial discourse. Hence, the issue of liberatory capacity lies in the subject's ability to possess language through manipulating and negotiating the systems of dispersion.

The Journey toward Becoming:
Historical Subjects and the Task of Translating Identity

Louisiana, by Erna Brodber, extends the project of examining authoritative discourses and the constructed knowledges which emerge as truths about historical subjects and their existence in the world. Brodber and Philip's projects are concerned with a similar problematic in Caribbean literature, that of ending the quarrel with history. Where Nourbese-Philip works from the assumption that language can "encapsulate, reflect and refine the entire experiential life and world view (*STHT*, 14), Brodber deconstructs the category of the real and the idea that the real presents itself through linguistic registers only. Brodber explores the possibility of reconstructing parts of the real, parts which have been subsumed through disciplinary acts such as dismembering, distancing, and alienating.

The relationship between literature and the positioning of subjects (and their subjectivity) is a problematic Brodber constantly wrestles with in her sociological research. This is more than an epistemological project for contemporary writers, for the stakes are nothing less than the very ground which situates the subject as an agent in its coming into becoming. As Edouard Glissant observes:

> The surface effects of literary realism are the precise equivalent of the historian's claim to pure objectivity. As opposed to the claim of describ-

ing *the whole of the real,* one might prefer the attempt to completely recon-
struct (or to recreate) in depth one part of this reality. Whatever the
case, man, not as agent but as will, had been placed at the center of the
literary and historical drama; the work often went no further than appearance, no deeper than the expression of this wish. To dig underneath, to reveal the inner workings, that is the aim of the kind of history
recently called sociological, and one must admit that this was the ambi-
tion behind the attempt of modern Western poets who became engaged
in bringing to light what was concealed *under the surface.*[11]

Glissant's description of the locale of the historical subject speaks
directly to the problematic that Nourbese-Philip identifies as "possession and legitimation." That is, for Glissant and writers like
Nourbese-Philip, the process of legitimation lies in the subject's ability to reach under the surface to reveal the systematic shifts and discursive ruptures inherent in discourses and to effect changes in the
manner in which the subject relates to the world around her.

My reading of Brodber's *Louisiana* participates in a theoretical intervention which adopts what I call a political theory of metaphysics.
This approach takes seriously the recent emphasis by cultural critics
on the arts of the imagination as more than an effort to be critical
of the creative process. This critical interest is more concerned with
redefining what constitutes the real (world) and what we define as
political within this context. Moreover, since the imagination is the
place where subjects first begin to conceive of the possibility of their
being, the boundaries that have historically confined colonial subjects (history in particular) take on different meanings. These meanings are no longer limited in their scope because of the preoccupation with the end result, but are invested with authority through the
very processes of thought engaged in by the thinking subject. The
political theory of metaphysics I am identifying attempts to move
current debates about the epistemological implications of comprehending difference as it relates to being and the constitution of subjectivity from a purely theoretical realm into an understanding of
the possibilities that lie beyond ontology.

Brodber's novel *Lousiana* is a reimagining of the relationship of
identity in the context of our understanding of being and its various
manifestations. Brodber is constructing a new discursive terrain, one
which, according to critics like Sylvia Wynter and Glissant, is essential for understanding the nature of existence for postmodern and
(arguably) postnationalist identities. Brodber focuses specifically on
situating being within the realm of the social and political, such that
the subject's becoming depends and is determined by her agency,

particularly when systems consist of constantly changing and duplic-
itous historical signifiers. Brodber has taken up the "condition" of
(non)existence in her works in an effort to dis-form institutionalized
discourses on difference and identity by closely examining the very
construction of these disciplinary discourses and their dissemination
across various social, cultural, and national boundaries. Just as earlier narratives, such as those represented in the literary journals *Trinidad* and *The Beacon*, grapple with the formation of a national identity and the necessity of producing an-other space for imagining an
alternative being, Brodber effectively combines these discursive ter-
rains, while bridging and exploding scientific discourses, in an effort
to construct an-other subject of history. By liberating subjects from
the underpinnings of the quarrel with history, Brodber effectively
sets the ground for a new mapping of the landscape of subjectivity,
constructed not merely by history, but in history.

Brodber's protagonist in her novel *Louisiana*, Ella Townsend, is a
literary descendant of Ella O'Grady, who appears in Brodber's second novel, *Myal*. Brodber's third novel is an important historical sequel to *Myal* that extends and complicates the epistemological problematics she is concerned with in *Myal*.[12] One such concern is the
necessity for colonial subjects to come into a knowledge of themselves born out of their own experiences and relationships with their
surroundings. *Myal* ends with an appeal from Ella, now a school
teacher who intervenes in the colonial education sytem for those
generations who will come after her, to take up the project of putting themselves back together through interior historical research:

> My people have been separated from themselves White Hen, by several
> means, one of them being the printed word and the ideas it carries. Now
> we have two people who are about to see through that. And who are
> these people, White Hen? People who are familiar with the print and the
> language of the print. Now, White Hen, now, we have people who can
> and are willing to correct images from the inside, destroy what should
> be destroyed, replace it with what it should be replaced with and put us
> back together, give us back ourselves with which to chart our course to
> go where we want to go.[13]

The protagonist in *Louisiana* takes up this challenge, as does
Brodber in the formal construction of her novel. Ella Townsend is a
graduate student, majoring in anthropology, who is sent to Louisiana to record the history of the "blacks of South West Louisiana," a
project which is supposedly geared toward putting back together the
lives of former slaves in the name of history. Ella is one of the up-

and-coming young black writers selected to work on the Works Project Administration, narratives begun by Franklin D. Roosevelt to organize and institutionalize knowledge about blacks in the United States. Ella is, potentially, one of the people *Myal*'s White Hen and her cohorts have identified as having the wherewithal to "correct images from the inside" (*M*, 109). The inside here refers to academic institutions, libraries, museums, and other hegemonic sites of knowledge production and dissemination. While *Myal*'s Ella O'Grady begins her examination into knowledge production in her primary school classroom, *Louisiana*'s Ella Townsend is a graduate student who conducts hers in the "field" of anthropology. Thus, *Louisiana* is part of an ongoing project for Brodber, one in which the stakes are defined in terms of the certainty of what is possible, not of what is assured. That is to say, Brodber's narrative strategies draw their political agency from the implied strength in the subject's willingness to undertake the task of thinking herself into existence. This act does not ensure an immediate change in the nature of existence for the subject. In this context, the narrative interest in Ella's actions is not directed at a particular ending but at a possible change in her current mode of being. The distinction here is significant for the connections between thinking and being in Brodber's narrative, as her narrative suggests that the possibility of coming into being lies in the subject's understanding of what thought makes possible.

Louisiana opens with a brief historical account of significant events in the United States during the 1930s. Constantly commenting upon itself as a narrative concerned with knowledge production and what constitutes the real, *Louisiana* brings historical texts into our line of vision as inherently questionable in their truth value. The "Editor's Note," therefore, works effectively to create a distance between the writer, the reader, and the distributor of this narrative. This distancing device both invests the project with a historical significance and situates the authority of the project in the hands of the historical subject. The text argues persuasively that Ella has come under the influence of psychic forces:

> Today the intellectual world understands that there are more ways of knowing than are accessible to the five senses; in 1936 when Ella Townsend received her assignment it was not so. The world is ready. We are. This manuscript's arrival is opportune. And in more than one way. (*M*, 109–10)

This opening claim marks the terrain for examining the scientific methods involved in retrieving "the history of the blacks of South

West Louisiana" by drawing our attention to our most dependable sources of recognition (scientific methods, recording equipment, firsthand accounts), only to highlight their limitations. The tape recorder as a primary tool of objectivity and accuracy is central to the Works Project Administration narratives. This machine, paired with proper fieldwork skills, was the primary means of assurance of objectivity in the WPA project.

We know from the "Editor's Note" that Ella, like many other writers, is selected for this project without much consideration of her own position as object/subject of the study in which she is involved. That is, she is chosen because she is black, and by virtue of her blackness, she is assumed to be an informant, or at least one who could readily gain entrance into this community and its history. This assumption is precisely what is at the heart of Brodber's metaphysical concerns. She contests the certainty of these assumptions by complicating the meanings of blackness in the American and the New World contexts. Moreover, she complicates our understanding of what it means to belong to a particular community by highlighting Ella's outsider status in St. Mary, Louisiana. Noting the shortcomings of Ella's book-learning, Mammy King reminds her that if she is to understand anything about blacks in Louisiana, she needs to first comprehend the connections between St. Mary, Jamaica and St. Mary, Louisiana:

> They teach Green Island 'bout Helen and Helena . . . see some of your pointless matter did stick in my head. One is a lady, the other is an island . . . But Green Island, they tell you nothing 'bout a place called Louisiana right here in these united states of America. Who laughs last . . . so Green Island jaw drop; Green Island now quiet. So hey there little green island, you ain't the only soul got a place called St. Mary, Louisiana. (*L*, 15)

The doubling of geographical and historical contexts in this passage provides the foundation for the cross-cultural migrations Brodber maps out during the course of her narrative. Mammy King's evocation of Greek mythology is meant to draw Ella's attention to the role of myth in covering over knowledge that presents itself for recognition, like the relationship between the island location, St. Mary, Jamaica, and the woman she is interviewing, Miss Anna (Louisiana), in St. Mary, Louisiana.

Ella believes (because she is told by the administrators of the WPA project) that she is coming to Louisiana to interview Mammy King, also known as Miss Anna (Louisiana), a former slave born and raised in St. Mary, Louisiana. Upon further inquiry, however, she is informed by Mammy King that her roots are in the island of Jamaica, St. Mary's parish. With this new bit of knowledge, Ella unconsciously embarks on a journey into her own becoming. The task of coming into being, through representing the presence of blacks as "lack," is complicated further by the claims of objective reporting in recording the stories of former slaves in Louisiana. Brodber, therefore, decides to deconstruct the category of history and the way in which it is supposed to function as an institutionalized discipline.

Brodber's return to the narratives of the Federal Writer's Project of the WPA is important in articulating this relationship between history and being. In the same vein as her contemporaries, Brodber engages the question of the production of being in the modern nation-state. The difference between the earlier Caribbean narratives and Brodber's approach to the questions of being and national identity lies in her revision of the foundational tropes for (en)gendering the nation, particularly with respect to geographical boundaries and political communities. Brodber's narrative draws upon the significant tropes of family, time, and progress only to turn them on their head by exposing the implicit agendas at work in projects such as the WPA narratives. Describing the historical function of these tropes in nation-building, Anne McClintock notes that:

> In the nineteenth century, the social evolutionists secularized time and placed it at the disposal of the national, imperialist project. The axis of *time* was projected onto the axis of *space*, and history became global. Now not only natural space but also historical time was collected, measured, and mapped onto a global science of the surface. In the process, history, especially national and imperial history, took on the character of a spectacle.[14]

McClintock describes the historical purpose of projects such as the WPA narratives. As Brodber suggests, the task of recording history depends largely on imposed uniformity and translations of events that rarely take into consideration the cultural contexts within which these events unfold. Ella's initial efforts to "translate" Mammy King is a prime example of this approach to recording history.

Brodber's protagonist, Ella Townsend, is drawn into an exploration of the forces which control reality by virtue of her academic endeavors as an anthropologist. Armed with her tape recorder, Ella starts out to record the life of one Mammy King, formerly known as Suzie Anna, from St. Mary, Louisiana. This project, for Mammy

King, however, holds a significantly different value from what Ella refers to as "these white people's history of the blacks in South West Louisiana" (*L*, 14). Mammy describes Ella's project as the "translation" of Mammy King. For Mammy King, this project represents her "coming over" to the other side, meeting her relatives who have died and gone over. The translation Mammy King envisions resembles a literal piecing together of various narratives, lives, geographies, and worlds toward the ends of articulating the processes which have brought her to this historical juncture in life. Mammy King's understanding of this project differs from Ella's in that she understands her translation to be a point of intersection between her former lives as a Jamaican immigrant and political activist.

As Ella continues to observe Mammy's musings, she begins to realize that these silences hold a history within themselves. As the collective narrative progresses, Ella's observations become more directed toward other forms of knowledge (psychic, sensory, and other worldly), and Mammy's various ploys and strategies for withholding information are deemed significant to Ella's induction:

> The child wrote down Anna's silence in her head as "full thick and deep."—Recording machine—, she said to herself,—I need braille to access these thoughts—Anna sighed another sigh that leaked out of our history and the girl made a note to be sure to find some way of transposing those sighs and those laughs and other non-verbal expressions of emotions into the transcript she would submit to her masters. (*L*, 14)

This recognition marks a significant shift in Ella's perception of her role as a social scientist because though her training tells her to write only what she is told, she recognizes that there are lessons to be learned from the unspoken, silenced spaces in Mammy's experiences. As the passage above suggests, there are several kinds of silences, all of which are open to a variety of interpretations. These silences include, but are not limited to, "unsaid" and "untold" stories; laughs and gestures which express ideas and emotions; voids, which at first appearance seem to be empty spaces; and articulations which render themselves in registers beyond Ella's interpretive strategies. The possibility for interpreting these silences depend largely on Ella's willingness to translate these instances into something other than what her training advises her to do, as something other than empty, inaudible corners of history.

As the narrative progresses, Mammy King's translation overwhelms Ella's historical project when she learns about the blacks in St. Mary, Louisiana. This knowledge brings Ella closer to her own presence in history and her family connections in Louisiana and St. Mary, Jamaica. However, just as Ella begins to make progress with her relationship with her "object of study," Mammy King dies, and she is faced with the prospect of the end of her project. When a voice from beyond instructs her to "just tell the white people the old lady has died," Ella realizes that this is just the beginning, not the end of her project (*L*, 27). For the first time Ella realizes that there is more to this project than recording the lives of blacks in Louisiana. Mammy King's death symbolizes a new challenge to Ella's historical project because she comes to understand that Mammy's death, like her life, involved more than could be contained in the WPA narratives.

Like Nourbese-Philip, Brodber brings a variety of discourses into dialogue with one another in order to make visible their interrelatedness. Where Nourbese-Philip achieves this by literally placing different literary genres on the same page, Brodber creates a similar effect by bringing all of these discourses in contact with one another in a field of free play which allows the productive capacities of the imagination to realize their potential. That is, Brodber's novel denies the rigidity of narrative rules: discussions between characters are quoted without any reference to who is speaking (suggesting a collective articulation); dialogues are not introduced; first-person narratives are void of any identification of the speaker. Her suggestion here is that the rules which govern narrative and performance shift, depending on the social-historical agendas at work in the construction of narratives of identity. This refusal to acknowledge boundaries extends to Brodber's own construction of academic, metaphysical, and geographical spaces, as is evidenced by the spirits of dead relatives who return to put their half of the story onto Ella's tape recorder.

What emerges from the novel is that historical projects such as the WPA narratives, rather than focusing on the lived experiences of blacks in the diaspora and the conscious relationship of subjects to their surroundings, depended on the authority of history as the instituting force of this new historical subjectivity. The emphasis on the construction of ex-slaves as witnesses and participants in history is significant to Brodber's revision of the scientific procedures involved in gathering information for the narratives. In *Louisiana*, Brodber addresses the (scientific and social) problematics of such an approach to the production of knowledge and subjectivity by recording the history of subjects in process, rather than assuming that the poles of subjecthood are always already stable, linear, and coherent in and through time. Brodber's project is to deconstruct conventional modes of reason with respect to realist narratives and the reality they are said to represent. The difficulty of maintaining the integrity of the reader/writer/subject in language and history is, for Brodber, an important site of free play from which the possibility for new modes of subject construction emerges.

The level of Brodber's engagement I am concerned with here, what I am calling a politics of metaphysics, is based on deconstructing discursive strategies which impose a reproductive relationship on the category of history. That Caribbean writers such as Erna Brodber, Marlene Nourbese-Philip, and others engage this project at the level of poetics is extremely significant. Brodber's first novel, *Jane and Louisa Will Soon Come Home*, Merle Collins's *The Colour of Forgetting*, Zee Edgell's *Beka Lamb*, and Merle Hodge's *Crick Crack Monkey*, for example, all propose similar projects aimed at articulating a female subject of history unbound from traditional binarisms which have historically confined the agency necessary for any sense of selfhood to emerge.

While all these narratives are concerned with the same epistemological concerns, each offers a different critical paradigm through which these concerns may be read and engaged. The works of Marlene Nourbese-Philip and Erna Brodber demonstrate that the subject's agency in producing itself needs to be understood and experienced at the level of a collective consciousness for it to have any relevance whatsoever. For, as these writers suggest, it is not simply at the level of experience that the subject realizes itself. It is through the nature of thinking and the possibilities that lie within this act that subjects realize and experience their being.

Notes

1. Lizabeth Paravisini and Barbara Webb, "On the Threshold of Becoming: Caribbean Women Writers," *Cimarron* 1, no. 3 (Spring 1988): 106.

2. See Evelyn O'Callaghan's "Early Versions: Outsiders' Voices/Silenced Voices," in *Woman Version: Theoretical Approaches to West Indian Fiction by Women* (London: Macmillan Caribbean, 1993), 17–35. O'Callaghan discusses ambivalent spaces occupied by early Caribbean women writers within the West Indian literary tradition. Some of the early twentieth-century writers she mentions include Elma Napier, Phyllis Shand Allfrey, and Jean Rhys (Dominica), Eliot Bliss and Alice Durie (Jamaica), and Celeste Dolphin (Guyana), all of whom were publishing fiction from the 1930s–1950s. See also Allison Donnell's "Difficult Subjects: Women's Writing in the Caribbean pre-1970" (paper, Sixth International Conference of Caribbean Women Writers and Scholars, Grenada, 1998).

3. Cornelius Castoriadis, *The Imaginary Institution of Society* (Cambridge, Mass.: MIT Press, 1987), 167.

4. O'Callaghan, *Woman Version*, 11.

5. My reference here is connected both to Caliban's assertion in *The Tempest*

that "this island's mine by Sycorax my mother" and to the popular idea of the "motherland" as the source of inspiration and contestation in many nationalist movements. This constructed space is not uniform in its conceptualizations but is nonetheless a common point of reference, as many of the cultural histories of Shakespeare's Caliban suggest. For two exhaustive historiographies of Shakespeare's Caliban and its various appropriations, see T. Alden and Virginia Mason Vaughan, *Shakespeare's Caliban: A Cultural History* (London: Cambridge University Press, 1991). See also, Roberto Fernández Retamar, *Caliban and Other Essays* (Minneapolis: University of Minnesota Press, 1989).

6. For example, in her collection of poetry, *Rotten Pomerack*, Merle Collins includes a poem entitled "No Dialects Please" in response to a call for submissions to a poetry contest. The advertisement, according to Collins, ended by stating that submissions in "dialects" would not be considered because, "after all we are British." The implicit assertion, that those who might speak or write in dialects— English dialects—were, first and foremost, not British and not a part of the British landscape would become a major obstacle facing Caribbean writers (particularly women) in Britain in the 1990s.

7. Martin Heidegger, *An Introduction to Metaphysics*, trans. Ralph Manheim (New Haven, Conn.: Yale University Press, 1959), 15–16.

8. Dionne Brand, a Trinidadian writing from Canada, raises these same issues in her collection of poetry, *No Language Is Neutral.*

9. Marlene Nourbese-Philip, *She Tries Her Tongue, Her Silence Softly Breaks* (Charlottesville, Canada: Ragweed Press, 1993), 56. Hereafter *STHT,* cited in the text.

10. Castoriadis, *Imaginary Institution of Society*, 354. Castoriadis borrows the phrase "leaning on" (*Anlehnung*) from Freudian psychoanalysis where it is used to designate the relationship between society and the "first natural stratum" or realm of the real as experienced in the unconscious. However, Castoriadis revises the term in his deployment so that the term takes on a more functional meaning. That is to say, for Castoriadis, the "leaning on" is not a passive act that occurs naturally. The "leaning on," far from being an end, is a means for changing the "first natural stratum."

11. Edouard Glissant, *Caribbean Discourse: Selected Essays* (Charlottesville: University Press of Virginia, 1989), 74.

12. Brodber has said on several occasions that her novels emerge from her sociological research at the Institute of Social and Economic Research, U.W.I., Mona, Jamaica. Her sociological research has centered on exploring the living conditions and possibilities for women in the Caribbean and include *Abandonment of Children in Jamaica* (1974), *A Study of Yards in the City of Kingston* (1975), and *Perceptions of Caribbean Women* (1984). What is clear in all of Brodber's works of fiction is her attempt to make the reality of social and historical conditions significant in such a way that the rules of functioning are brought to the surface of this reality, brought back into the realm of that which is experienced.

13. Erna Brodber, *Myal* (London and Port of Spain: New Beacon Books, 1992), 109–10. Hereafter *M,* cited in the text.

14. Anne McClintock, *Imperial Leather* (New York: Routledge, 1995), 92.

Struggling with a Structure: Narrating Gender and Agency across Discursive Boundaries

Glyne Griffith
Bucknell University

> Generally speaking, intelligence and imagination become premium modalities of functional existence to a people who are traditionally perceived as hewers of wood, drawers of water and mere statistical units in the production process.
> —Rex Nettleford, *Inward Stretch, Outward Reach*

I N this essay I am concerned with examining some of those discursive strategies employed by the earth's wretched to make intelligence and imagination function as premium modalities of existence so that personhood and humanity may be rescued from the alienating and destructive forces of domination. If, for example, particular readings and interpretations of race and gender are pressed into the service of domination, how might various strategies which privilege intelligence and imagination, in contradistinction to the "thingification" processes of domination, serve to establish the agency of those who would otherwise languish as mere units of labor, existing more as thing than person?

The first part of the title, "Struggling with a Structure," is meant to signal the essay's concern with the ways in which narrative and discursive structures can either enhance or limit attempts to read through dehumanizing strategies of domination so that one may establish agency and humanity. Thus one struggles with narrative and discursive structures as part of the praxis of liberatory struggle. In addition, the first part of the title has an anecdotal aspect which will lead into the main discussion. Several years ago when I lived in Jamaica, a Rastafari friend concluding a conversation with me indicated that he was on his way to express his amorous intentions to a woman whom he had recently met. In his own words, he indicated to me that he was on his way to "struggle with a structure." His obvious objectification of the woman's personhood in his syntactic choice of "structure" was as interesting as his representation of the impending encounter as a "struggle." Despite my friend's clear confidence in his own persuasive and rhetorical skills, he expected to be challenged, to meet resistance to his amorous advances. In addition, his choice of the term "structure" to represent the object of his desire seemed to suggest the formidable otherness that he understood womanhood to be. He was going to encounter resistance to the manifestation of his will, and rendered through his discursive lens, it was as though this resistance lacked particular agency and subjectivity. It was, rather, an undistinguished background of feminine complexity, an ontological canvas upon which his assured masculine subjectivity and agency would assert itself and achieve central focus.

Somehow, though, I suspect that what my friend had perceived to be an impending encounter with a "drawer of water," if not a "hewer of wood," probably turned into an encounter with "intelligence and imagination" displayed as a "premium modality of this woman's functional existence," for I don't recall him ever mentioning the outcome of the encounter. His utter silence on the matter might be read, if we move from the particular idiosyncrasy of this anecdote to speak more generally of weightier narratives of dominance and power, as a kind of silencing of other narratives, other modes of knowing and being in the world. As such, the modalities of existence and indeed resistance of which Rex Nettleford speaks in the epigraph above[1] are likely to tend toward subterfuge and subversion since they are so typically marginalized and silenced by dominant strategies of knowing and being.

The intelligence of these putative statistical units of labor, these voiceless subalterns, will likely invest in ways of knowing and existing that undermine and resist conservatively established boundaries, norms, and limits. Such disenfranchised imagination often challenges narrative and discursive efforts to represent knowledge and truth as entirely resident within the discrete borders of established disciplines, accessible only through sanctioned discursive and disciplinary practices. Intellectually sensitive and liberatory analyses of such intelligence and imagination thus demand disciplinary and epistemological border-crossings which explore the conceptual terrain between putative borders and discrete polarities. Such border-crossings that explore intelligence, imagination, and agency where they have been said not to exist have been facilitated and enhanced by theoretical and critical practices such as poststructuralism and

postcolonial theory. Perhaps we might usefully think of the prefix
"post" in both these cases as referring less to the idea that we have
clearly moved beyond dominant structures of ordering and knowing
in the world, or that we have moved beyond relations in the geo-
political world which still bear the mark of colonialism, and instead
understand the "post" to speak more properly of the impossibility
nowadays of thinking of the suffixes in any unselfconscious manner.

Although poststructuralist critique has been viewed with more
than a healthy skepticism in some academic circles, both in the Caribbean and internationally, it is clear that there is value in what it
has revealed about knowledge, the conditions and strategies of
knowing, and the nature of truth. The destabilizing force of deconstructive analysis, for example, facilitates an iconoclastic hermeneutic so that so-called master narratives are seen to have always contained the condition of their own unraveling because they have
always established themselves against resistances. Deconstructive
analysis, for example, tends to represent knowing as the ever-shift-
ing intersection of knowing and not knowing rather than as a discrete bifurcation of knowledge (truth) and nonsense (falsehood).
Indeed, a number of poststructuralism's detractors fault precisely
this tendency to render every discursive position unstable and provisional as being one of poststructuralism's most dissatisfying traits,
but arguably this tendency toward the provisional and the unstable
is part of its attractiveness as a discursive weapon of the weak. Since
deconstructive analysis, for example, tends to focus attention on
what is rendered inadmissible in the so-called master narrative, on
what has to remain unsaid and outside the boundaries of a discourse
so that the discourse may maintain a stereotypical coherence, it per-
mits us to ask questions about the assumptions and premises which
ground a dominant narrative and create the occasion and possibility
for speaking.

One of the distinct advantages of literature is that as a discipline
its practices and boundaries tend to be less easily and rigidly defined
than several other disciplines in the humanities or social sciences.
Commenting on the deconstructive possibilities in literary discourse, Gayatri Spivak notes the significant difference between literary discourse and discourses within several other disciplines which
fall under the rubric of the humanities or the social sciences. She
states:

> Whereas in other kinds of discourses there is a move toward the final
> truth of a situation, literature . . . displays that the truth of a human situa-
> tion is the itinerary of not being able to find it. In the general discourse

of the humanities, there is a sort of search for solutions, whereas in literary discourse there is a playing out of the problem as the solution.[2]

This playing out of the problem as the solution undermines discursive tendencies associated with metaphysical binarism and what Jacques Derrida has referred to as a "logocentric metaphysics." Generally, the interplay between literature and poststructuralist critique, as well as the interplay between black diaspora literatures and the history of plantation slavery in the so-called New World, can lead to a profound sense that, as Spivak indicates: "all conclusions are genuinely provisional and therefore inconclusive, that all origins are similarly unoriginal, that responsibility itself must cohabit with frivolity."[3]

The movement away from discursive strategies which aim to find a final, absolute truth, and toward the adoption of strategies which focus on the itinerary of narrative rather than its arrival at some epistemological or ontological destination, has value for analyses within studies such as those referenced above. Deconstructive readings question essentialist definitions and thus facilitate the recognition of contradictory and resistant forces within discourses predicated upon stereotype and the movement toward some final truth of the human situation. Strategies of resistance to essentializing discourses which seek their salvation in oppositional but similarly binarist practices, such as for example, the location of selfhood within essentialist narratives of negritude or afrocentricity or nationalism, in the attempt to counter the degradation of personhood under colonialist or imperialist domination, are severely limiting if they are not recognized as provisional stages in a continuing struggle against the limitations of binarist structures of knowing and being.

Some modes of feminist critique, for example, have demonstrated awareness of the ontological cul-de-sac of essentialism. Thus, Spivak, recognizing the fallacy of essentialist configurations within gender, argues that:

My own definition of a woman is very simple: it rests on the word "man" as used in the texts that provide the foundation for the corner of the literary criticism establishment that I inhabit. You might say at this point, defining the word "woman" as resting on the word "man" is a reactionary position. Should I not carve out an independent definition for myself as a woman? . . . The only way that I can see myself making definitions is in a provisional and polemical one: I construct my definition as a woman not in terms of a woman's putative essence but in terms of words currently in use. "Man" is such a word in common usage.[4]

Spivak's definition of woman, not in terms of some putative essence, but grounded in the tension between the binarism of "Man" and "Woman," destabilizes any discursive essentializing of "Man." In short, her construction of "Woman" in relative rather than essentialist terms simultaneously undermines attempts to narrate "Man" in essentialist rather than relativist terms. As indicated already, one of the discursive advantages of literature is that as a discipline its boundaries are not too strictly defined. In addition, as Spivak suggests, literary discourse tends to tease out the several representations of a problem as a solution itself, rather than seek some final solution in attempts at discursive closure. These disciplinary characteristics are advantageous on a number of levels, and I would like to ground what I have been saying thus far by engaging in a commentary on two narratives which might be said to be in "the margins" of those two narratives in order to focus on aspects of black agency and gender construction in a plantation slavery and postemancipation, colonial context.

The texts I have chosen are Hilary Beckles's historical narrative, *Natural Rebels: A Social History of Enslaved Black Women in Barbados,* and Earl Lovelace's novel, *The Wine of Astonishment.* Both narratives struggle with the challenge of representing a historically and ontologically degraded black Caribbean personhood and womanhood. The challenge or struggle (recalling the first part of this essay's title) which these two narratives engage is twofold. There is the discursive challenge of locating and privileging human agency against a formidable hegemony that would deny such volition and agency. In addition, there is the danger of remaining within the conceptual trap of metaphysical binarism, simply inverting stereotypical polarities in the attempt to represent the agency of the wretched of the earth. We will look at the strategies employed by each narrative and try to guage the relative efficacy of each.

Beckles's historical narrative is involved in a disciplinary struggle with a fairly conservative Caribbean historiography. His narrative is challenged to represent a history of black female slave resistance and rebellion in Barbados against a background of historical documentation and archival sources which are, for the most part, not constitutive of the slave as agent and even less constitutive of the agency of the female slave. How, therefore, might such a narrative retrieve a doubly silenced voice from archival representations which retain the ideological accretions of Enlightenment and imperialist delimitations of reason and humanity and still remain within the disciplinary boundaries and narrative conventions of history? How does such a narrative satisfactorily represent black female slave resistance,

drawing upon statistical documentation which overlays that iconoclastic intelligence and imagination of which Nettleford speaks,
without losing sight of these premium modalities of black female
functional existence?

The challenge for *Natural Rebels* is to account historically for the
survival, development, and manifestation of black slave women's resistance strategies in the face of a brutal and oppressive victimization
in Barbadian plantation slave society. The narrative might also be
said to be an implicit discussion of gender construction informed by
metaphysical binarism, but more will be said of this later. There is a
contradictoriness in the narrative of *Natural Rebels* which is evidenced as early as the work's introduction. This contradictoriness is
a consequence of disruptive sites in the progression of the historical
tale because irony, ambivalence, and ambiguity, more convention-
ally associated with literariness, inheres in the telling of the tale. The
narrative reads against itself, in a manner of speaking, as it struggles
with its own structure. It is a struggle between the discourse of a conservative historiography and a polemical narrative desire to narrate
black female slave agency out of the otherness decreed it by historical oppression and a conservative historiography. In effect, this discursive struggle produces between the covers of *Natural Rebels* a sort
of schizophrenic narrative, a type of embattled "two-ness" reminiscent of W. E. B. DuBois's use of that phrase.[5] The text functions as a
struggle between disciplinary desire to remain within the borders of
history and discursive desire to imaginatively narrate black female
agency out of the dehumanizing underbelly of plantation slave society in Barbados. The work's introduction presents the earliest evidence of the conflict which will ensue. Beckles writes:

> The forces of oppression and resistance are paramount throughout, as
> their dimensions emerge forcefully from the evidence. Rarely do the
> data express the actual views of women, and this represents one of the
> primary difficulties encountered in writing. Psycho-historical methods
> and techniques have not yet taken root in Caribbean historiography, and
> scholars are now acutely aware that existing methods are limited in
> terms of reaching behind plantation-based data and into the daily lives
> of slaves.[6]

Thus the task of *Natural Rebels* is to represent the "natural rebelliousness" of black slave women in Barbados and yet remain within
the boundaries of traditional historical discourse, leaning heavily on
historical evidence. As a result, the work's introduction prepares the
reader to read against the grain of the overwhelmingly statistical and

demographic data presented in the narrative. The reader is challenged to reach behind plantation-based data in order to read rebelliousness into a narrative of historical evidence which would traditionally seek because of the particular epistemological and ontological constraints informing the evidence to negate such narratives of resistance. In reaching behind the statistical data to read the natural rebelliousness of these slave women, the reader is perhaps inadvertently led to ponder whether the naturalness of this female rebellion is the product of that "always already" resistance which is coexistent with the will-to-dominance, or whether it is the by-product of metaphysical binarism, an ahistorical, asocial naturalness to be associated, within the binarism of gender, in other words, with woman's otherness.

Frequently in *Natural Rebels*, reaching behind or reading into the putative master narrative of historical evidence to recognize resistance demands that the surface narrative of historical evidence be read as a continuous metaphor, standing in, as metaphors do, for the narrative of resistance which lies submerged beneath the historical data. The early sections of *Natural Rebels* indicate, for example, that bell hooks, Klein, Mannix, and Cowley acknowledge that:

> it is very difficult for scholars to express in the language of the social sciences the results of the sexual exploitation, infection, nutritional deficiency, daily observation of death and sickness, and the physical torture that characterized the middle passage. But all generally agree that those women who did survive as healthy individuals possessed extraordinary abilities and capacities. (*NR*, 28)

This inference, derived from what can be said within the domain of social science language or available historical evidence, offers a glimpse of a subtext which is arguably twice repressed by the hegemonic discourse of those who have the capacity to speak and represent authoritatively, on the one hand, and by disciplinary boundaries and procedures which impose additional discursive restrictions, on the other. If we assume that part of the difficulty of expressing slave women's humanity and agency in the language of the social sciences results from the distancing and objectification consequent on empirical and statistical representation, is there a potential risk of narrating that humanity and rebelliousness within the stereotypical confines of metaphysical binarism, even as one seeks to reach behind the plantation-based data? In other words, is the intelligence and imagination which resists mere statistical commodification of human existence qualitatively different as a result of gender?

Part of the difficulty with which *Natural Rebels* seems to struggle is the location of the source of black slave women's rebelliousness. It is probable that this results, inter alia, from the narrative's attempt to suggest slave women's more profound brutalization and consequent subjugation as a result of gender, while simultaneously acknowledging that in the plantation fields little attention was paid to gender difference. In the second chapter of the text, for example, the narrative draws on historical data and indicates both the slavers' perception of female cargo as potentially more docile than male cargo, as well as the increased likelihood of successfully induced female docility because of the potential for more effective brutalization of female cargo: "Voyage reports show that women, unlike men, experienced less policing on deck—the result of slavers' perception of them as the less dangerous part of the cargo" (*NR*, 27). In addition, we read in the same chapter, entitled "Field Women: Beasts of Burden," a quotation drawn from bell hooks's work:

> The traumatic experiences of African women and men aboard slave ships were only the initial stages of an indoctrination process that would transform the African free human being into a slave. An important part of the slaver's job was to effectively transform the African personality aboard the ships so that it would be marketable as a "docile" slave . . . African females received the brunt of this mass brutalization and terrorization not only because they could be victimized via their sexuality, but also because they were more likely to work intimately with white families than black males. (*NR*, 27–28)

The foregoing would seem to suggest either a presumed predisposition to docility as a result of being female or the slavers' greater success with enforced docility because of the female slave's arguably increased susceptibility to brutalization as a result of her gender. We might place these observations against, say, Bridget Brereton's critique, in a review of *Natural Rebels*, as well as against Barbara Bush's arguments in *Slave Women in Caribbean Society, 1650–1838* or Marieta Morrissey's *Slave Women in the New World: Gender Stratification in the Caribbean*. Brereton's conclusion is consonant with the acknowledgment made by these other historians:

> On the sugar plantations of the Caribbean, women slaves were mostly field labourers, and they performed all the heaviest, most monotonous tasks of planting, cultivation and harvesting, as well as the unskilled jobs around the mill. Managers had no qualms about employing women in heavy field tasks (concepts about the "gentler" sex had no relevance to

slaves) and gender differentiation in the field was minimal, except for concessions made to pregnant and nursing women after the 1780s.[7]

Since these narratives seem to be in agreement that in the Caribbean women slaves were mostly field laborers, and that, as Brereton adds, "so far as field labor was concerned, the plantation regime paid little attention to gender differentiation and, in this sense, plantation slavery was 'gender blind,' " we might usefully consider whether the gender differentiation which is so crucial to the polemic of *Natural Rebels* is really a consequence of the narrative's self-conscious desire to reach behind plantation-based data or a result of the narrative's own unselfconscious, binarist conceptualization of gender. That is to say, if the majority of female slaves in Caribbean plantation society tended to be employed in the field, where we are told gender differentiation was minimal, might it not be more strategic for *Natural Rebels* to focus its critical lens on these women who represented the majority as it searches for the rebelliousness of Barbadian slave women? In its attempt to reach behind plantation-based data, might the narrative not also have usefully attempted to reach behind patriarchy's bifurcation of gender attributes and dependence on stereotypical representations of femininity? Rather, the narrative tends to seek slave women's resistance, not only among that minority group which worked in areas other than the field, but seems to focus its examination of slave women's resistance and rebelliousness in stereotypically gendered locales associated with domesticity and nurturing.

Certainly, chapters one and two of *Natural Rebels*, titled "Outnumbering Men: A Demographic Survey" and "Field Women: Beasts of Burden," respectively, begin with some discussion of slave women's general abuse as chattel and units of labor in the plantation field, but the narrative does not begin to explore and discover slave women's resistance in any significant manner until we reach those chapters which address issues of domesticity and the plantation's routine exploitation of slave women's reproductive capacity. Although it is important to locate aspects of slave women's resistance strategies in the context of female sexuality and its abuse, it is equally important that the excavation of these strategies of resistance does not too quickly satisfy itself by resting on a foundation of metaphysical binarism and stereotypically gendered differentiation. Such would-be rebellious narratives need to avoid the ontological fallacy embraced, for example, by Shakespeare's Lady Macbeth when she implores:

> Come, you spirits
> That tend on mortal thoughts, unsex me here;
> And fill me, from the crown to the toe, top-full
> Of direst cruelty. Make thick my blood,
> Stop up th'access and passage to remorse,
> That no compunctious visitings of nature
> Shake my fell purpose nor keep peace between
> Th'effect and it. Come to my woman's breasts,
> And take my milk for gall, you murd'ring ministers,
> Wherever in your sightless substances
> You wait on nature's mischief.
>
> *(Macbeth* 1. 5. 37–47)

Did slave women need to "unsex" themselves to meet the cruel dehumanization of slavery with equally cruel resistance strategies? Did the lack of significant gender differentiation in the plantation field or resistance acts such as infanticide make slave women less self-consciously female? Was a stereotypical discharge of femininity the primary context in which slave women found the opportunity for resistance? *Natural Rebels* would seem to inadvertently imply as much. For example, in chapter three, entitled "House Women: The Privileged Few," the narrative recounts, among other details, the story of Old Doll, a domestic slave and her family at Newton plantation in Barbados. The narrative, employing evidence from the Newton plantation papers, indicates that Old Doll, her three daughters and niece enjoyed a relatively privileged status as household labor rather than field labor and that they did what they deemed necessary to ensure, as far as possible, the continuation of such relative privilege. We learn, for example, that a significant strategy of resistance employed by Old Doll's family resided in the family's relative freedom over its own reproductive capacity:

> As Doll's family consolidated its status as housekeepers, its members also became increasingly whiter as a result of miscegenation. Wood noted that all the girls "either have or have had white husbands, that is, men who keep them" . . . The records do not suggest that they had any relations with slave men, but such relations seem unlikely given the women's perceptions of elitism, authority, and self-esteem. *(NR,* 67)

To the extent that Doll and female members of her family use their relative positions of privilege in the plantation household to consolidate their social status within a white slaveholding plantocracy, we can legitimately question some of their actions as acts of resistance, and yet it appears that the narrative voice in *Natural Rebels* seeks precisely to represent their actions, including their response to miscegenation, as bona fide acts of resistance:

> the overall image which emerges is one of women—mothers and grandmothers—struggling to improve the intellectual and material lot of their families against reactionary plantation policies and constraints imposed by the wider slave system. (*NR*, 68)

Indeed, chapter 3 concludes with the following observation:

> Based on economic and social indicators, and on their own and their infants' mortality rate, house women were part of the labor elite. Nobody knew the true value attached to this status better than house women themselves, though the clue possibly lies in the fact that many would rather risk life and limb in resistance than be sent back to the fields. (*NR*, 70)

Here, the concept of resistance has less to do with the subversion of normative stereotypes than with acquiescence to the dictates of white slaveholding plantocratic socialization. Old Doll and her family survived, but if resistance by slave women such as Doll and the female members of her family can be so readily characterized as doing whatever was expedient to lighten the skin of progeny or to avoid being returned to field labor, might we not assume that on occasion such resistance would have been at the expense of those other women who remained in the field and who constituted the majority of slave women on Newton plantation? Might we not justifiably call for a distinction, despite the often thin line separating the two, between individualistic and purely self-interested strategies of social and material survival, and a form of resistance which aimed at benefiting the wider, disenfranchised group? More importantly, a narration of slave women's resistance which appears to give pride of place to slave women's commitment to the plantocracy's ideals of whiteness, family, motherhood, and nurture, within the ontological contradictoriness of plantation slavery, severely limits the discursive space available to the narrative to represent those slave women's resistance which might have been rooted in androgyny and infanticide, positions ideologically opposed to the plantocracy's idealization of womanhood and family. As Elizabeth Fox-Genovese argues, for example:

> All cultures have valued motherhood, but nineteenth-century bourgeois culture raised it to unprecedented heights of sentimentality and thus made it especially difficult for women to tell stories about its dangers

and conflicts. Bourgeois idealization of mothers' natural inclinations for nurture and self-sacrifice virtually prohibited women [or men] from writing realistically from a subjective stance. Or, to put it differently, the sanctity that shrouded the conventions of motherhood virtually dictated that women would have to embrace prescribed motherly feelings when writing of their own emotions or experience.[8]

Thus, a discourse which frames slave women's resistance in stereo-typically gendered terms, reading femininity as that essential other-ness and opposite of masculinity, is likely to locate female resistance at the center of patriarchal gaze and desire, consequently losing sight of struggle and resistance occurring at the periphery of such masculine-centered vision. In a brief but insightful commentary on Toni Morrison's *Beloved* as hybrid, historical text, for example, Fox-Genovese considers the ways in which Morrison's narrative breaks some of the silences and bridges some of the gaps which are often insufficiently rendered in typical historical readings of female slave struggle and resistance. The focus of the narrative in *Beloved* is the struggle of slaves to exist and grasp for their humanity on the Sweet Home plantation in Kentucky. Sethe, one of the novel's central characters, manifests that cruel conviction which Lady Macbeth sought unsuccessfully in Shakespeare's tragedy, not for personal am-bition, but in order to continue to exist as human agent. As Fox-Genovese indicates:

> The figure of Sethe, standing in the woodshed, dripping with the blood of the murdered baby girl, whose body she will not relinquish, offering her blood-dripping nipple to the surviving infant, challenges any recog-nizable image of motherhood. ("UTU," 12)

Sethe's act of infanticide is imaginatively rendered in Morrison's narrative in an attempt to reach behind plantation-based data, re-calling Beckles's admonishment, to represent the agency and ironi-cally the humanity of the slave mother. Simultaneously, Morrison's sustained and intimate focus on Sethe's act of infanticide narrates the "outside" of the historical narrative, the unspeakable act which a conservative historiography cannot sanction as utterance and re-main within the traditional boundaries of the discipline. As Fox-Genovese reminds us:

> Beloved, the ghost of the murdered, "crawling already?" baby remains not lost, but disremembered and unaccounted for, because no one is even looking for her. The story of her murder by her own mother, which implicated slavery in its entirety, including the other members of the

community of slaves, was not one that anyone—black or white, slave or
free—chose to tell. So they forgot. And their forgetting, even more than
the original event, becomes a story that cannot be passed on. ("UTU,"
1)

Thus, as the narrative struggles to utter the unspeakable, to tell its
tale, it is also struggling with its manner of telling and it is struggling
with discursive structures.

The questions that narratives are allowed to ask, the ways in which
their prevailing discourse allows them to frame their subject, will
have significance for what those narratives are finally able to say,
whether the topic is Caribbean slave women's resistance or the plantation economy's configurations of gender. Beckles's *Natural Rebels*
implicitly recognizes that the intelligence and imagination of which
Nettleford speaks in *Inward Stretch, Outward Reach* must be privileged
in order to bring the humanity and agency of the black female slave
to visibility, but the text seems insufficiently self-conscious of its own
discursive indebtedness to binarist conceptions of gender. As a consequence, the narrative does not manage to fully explicate its tale of
resistance and agency even though Beckles, as a historian, is willing
to employ the historical imagination. As Brereton indicates in her
review of *Natural Rebels*:

> Both Beckles and [Barbara] Bush suggest that the historian of Carib-
> bean slavery must try to transcend these difficulties [that is to say, the
> paucity of "hard" archival evidence] by the use of "historical imagina-
> tion" and "empathy." Beckles writes: "At times it is necessary for histori-
> ans to distance themselves from documents which purport to speak for
> slaves and look directly at what the slaves were in fact doing . . . The data
> deficiency can be compensated for by looking at the actions of women
> in their everyday lives." ("SIW," 87)

While such hermeneutic strategies are indeed required, it is also
true that there is no looking *directly* at what the slaves were doing;
there is no unmediated embrace of fact and truth. Part of my argument, therefore, is that the discursive strategy which *Natural Rebels*
employs to excavate the ontologically subterranean agency of black
female slave life in Barbados is insufficiently aware of its own indebtedness to a stereotypically binarist reading of gender.

As a result, the narrative participates in the inadvertent "othering" of the feminine, and consequently loses sight of strategies of
female slave resistance, rebellion, and agency which might not have
been grounded in the normative femininity and dominant discourse
of the plantation house, but might have been unearthed in the un-

sexed, androgynous conditions demanded of the field and antima-
ternal acts such as infanticide.

Let us turn our attention now to a fictional work which also employs the historical imagination to grapple with difficulties similar to
those addressed by *Natural Rebels*. Earl Lovelace's *The Wine of Astonishment* is a narrative which implicitly recognizes that imperialist
and patriarchal discourses are intricately intertwined. Lovelace's
novel is discursively consonant with narratives such as Morrison's *Beloved*, for example. Although Lovelace's novel takes the postemancipation, colonial period rather than the plantation slavery period as
its convenient historical moment, its discursive exploration of gender construction and human agency renders it a suitable choice for
comparison with *Natural Rebels*.

The Wine of Astonishment is an imaginative account of the struggles
of black Trinidadian members of the Shouter Baptist church, whose
religious practices were proscribed by British colonial government
law on 28 November 1917. In the narrative representation of anticolonial resistance, Lovelace's text also subverts a stereotypical bifurcation of gender attributes, and this strategy is crucial to the narrative's overall representation of Afro-Trinidadian struggle and
agency. The novel uses its antibinarist reading of gender to imaginatively represent the resistance of peoples, conservatively constituted
as the passive victims of colonialism and Empire. Indeed, European
imperialism's representation of its "subject races" constituted these
peoples in terms quite similar to patriarchy's problematic rendering
of woman and the feminine. Thus Lovelace's narrative seems implicitly to recognize that any adequate representation of the agency of
the colonized subject necessitates an anti-imperialist critique of gender. At one level, *The Wine of Astonishment* might be said to dramatize,
in the context of early twentieth-century Trinidad, the following
general observation of gender and Empire made by Ashis Nandy:

> Since about the seventeenth century, the hyper-masculine over-social-
> ized aspects of European personality had been gradually supplanting the
> cultural traits which had become identified with femininity, childhood,
> and later on, "primitivism." As part of a peasant cosmology, these traits
> had been valued aspects of a culture not wedded to achievement and
> productivity. Now they had to be rejected as alien to mainstream Euro-
> pean civilization and projected on to the "low cultures" of Europe and
> on to the new cultures European civilization encountered. It was as part
> of this process that the colonies came to be seen as the abode of people
> childlike and innocent on the one hand, and devious, effeminate and
> passive-aggressive on the other.[9]

In light of Nandy's observation, it is interesting to note the dramatization of the struggle between what he labels the hyper-masculine, over-socialized personality of colonial power and the passive-aggressive personality of colonial resistance, as rendered in Lovelace's novel. Implicitly recognizing the limitedness of binarist strategies of gender construction, particularly in terms of establishing resistance narratives, Lovelace's narrative oscillates between binarist polarities as it attempts to offer an interdependent representation of gender in an Afro-Trinidadian, postemancipation context.

The traits which the English colonizers associated with a peasant cosmology are represented in Lovelace's narrative by the Shouter Baptist faithful who reside in rural Bonasse. Eva, the narrator of events, has a keen sense of herself as an individual, but she also possesses a strong sense of community values. Her husband, Bee, is the pastor of the Baptist church and he tries his utmost to bridge the ever-widening gulf between the old folkways of Bonasse and the new urban-oriented dispensation, sanctioned by the English colonial authorities and fervently touted by a few villagers such as Ivan Morton and Mitchell. However, it is the village stick fighter, Bolo, who most fully represents the devalued and oppressed peasant culture of which Nandy speaks.

Bolo's sensitivity, in addition to his physical prowess and decisiveness as a stick fighter in the gayelle, personify those traits which Nandy argues were rejected by eurocentric colonial ideology and projected onto so-called low cultures. Bolo also represents a subversion of stereotypical gender attributes founded upon the restrictiveness of binary oppositions. Early in the narrative, Lovelace has his narrator, Eva, describe Bolo:

> this Bolo was a special man; and not only to us, the women, to everybody. If you have a house to build or a dead to bury, you could call him to lend a hand, and though he's a man who fears nobody, he knows how to laugh, and if you down to cheer you up, and he could feel sorry.[10]

As the narrative progresses, Bolo is seen to internalize stereotypical masculine and feminine attributes as a complex unity rather than as mutually antagonistic, binarist principles. Indeed, it is not really that Bolo is an "alienated idealist," as Marjorie Thorpe suggests in her introduction to the 1983 Heinemann edition of the novel, but rather that he is a living reflection of the village's peasant cosmology, an overarching presence which embodies their past. As such, Bolo's presence and his actions force the village community and the eurocentric ideologues to examine the falsehood of ontological

strategies of blackness and personhood grounded in a discrete sepa-
ration of male and female principles. Bolo embodies both principles, whereas the police corporal, Prince, exhibits the hyper-masculine behavior which meets the approval of the authorities whom he
serves, and thus he is one of the destabilizing forces in the village,
challenging the villager's peasant notions of masculinity, africanity,
and agency. Prince's overdetermined masculinity makes him devoid
of compassion and thus Eva describes him as:

> Tall, stocky as a gru-gru tree, this policeman show no sympathy or re-
> spect or mercy for people black like he. He was the law. The whiteman
> send him to do a job, and he do it, like a tank or a tractor or an elephant
> gone mad, bowling over and uprooting and smashing without human
> compassion or reasoning. (*WA*, 35–36)

Eva describes Prince as an automaton, lacking "compassion or
reasoning" and thus lacking humanity and the capacity for agency.
Thus, when Bolo tells the villagers that Prince must be killed, he is
attempting to reestablish in village life an equilibrium of masculine
and feminine principles. In other words, Prince is engaged in hyper-
masculine behavior in the sense outlined by Nandy in his analysis of
an overdetermined, destructive masculinity. Femininity, represented as the necessary and subordinate otherness of an overdetermined masculinity, is repressed in the discourse of the dominant
group and projected onto the politically and economically disenfranchised group. Bolo implicitly recognizes that in their response
to the repressive state power, the villagers of Bonasse have been emphasizing the hyper-feminine traits projected onto them as subjects
of Empire. Their reaction to the oppressive hyper-masculinity of the
colonial establishment, represented in the novel by Prince, is characterized by behavior consistent with hyper-femininity, epitomized
by the character Primus. Such reaction traps them in the stereotyped otherness of metaphysical binarism and reinforces the establishment daydream that such subject-races are indeed civilization's
rejects. Bolo intuitively understands this imperialist context and
struggles against such a destructive worldview.

The village men speak of deliberations with the colonial officials,
although they know that this is futile. Stick fighting, that symbol of
village warriorhood, has become a caricature where the faint of
heart take up handkerchiefs in Buntin's bar and challenge the legendary Bolo to a choreographed display of manhood. Bolo asserts
his manhood, not as a deferral of stereotypically feminine traits, but
in an attempt to reestablish gender equilibrium in the collective psy-

che of the village. Significantly, at the point in the narrative where Bolo admonishes the villagers to kill Prince, Lovelace has his narrator Eva provide an assessment of the village men's discomfort with Bolo's suggestion. Eva's narrative comment highlights her own compassion and restraint when faced with the prospect of Bolo's suggestion that the villagers should kill Prince. It is a compassion and restraint stereotypically associated with motherhood and nurture, but Eva also expresses some exasperation at the villager's continued passivity, and as a consequence of this exasperation, she gives greater resonance to the efficacy of Bolo's position and thus she draws closer to Sethe's atypical motherhood in *Beloved*. Even if not poised to kill as Sethe does, Eva seems at least willing to injure, to maim. She muses:

> In a woman's way, I could understand why these men don't know what to say. I know as well as they that we talk to the authorities already and that ain't solve nothing and the main thing to do should be . . . I wouldn't say kill. No not kill Prince, but at least do something to make him feel . . . But I know this is not a easy thing for them to decide to do. And I don't mean that they not brave. The men have to think about more than their bravery. Because once you start against the police, you have to continue. So I know is something they have to give proper consideration to; but even so, I agree with Sister Ruth when she say, "But we talk to them already, and they never listen. What they expect us to do?" (*WA*, 38)

Eva's recollection of Sister Ruth's cryptic "What they expect us to do?" hints at her own exasperation in the face of corporal Prince's draconian measures and Ivan Morton's feeble representation of village interests in the government council. Eva's compassion and restraint become aligned with Bolo's recognition that assertive force is necessary. She agrees with Sister Ruth that all other avenues have been exhausted, and at this point in the narrative there is concord between Eva's association with stereotypically feminine traits and Bolo's association with stereotypically masculine traits. Thus the reading which Lovelace's narrative makes possible in the context of feminine and masculine attributes is that compassion and nurture are not always antithetical to destruction, and destructiveness is not always necessarily devoid of compassion and nurture.

Both Prince and Ivan Morton in their eagerness to be efficient instruments of colonial power repress those qualities and traits associated with nurture and compassion. Ivan Morton's rejection of Eulalie, the village belle and the woman whose femininity is characterized as complementary to Bolo's masculinity, is a symbolic rejection of village belief and tradition. Indeed, Eulalie's fascination with Ivan Morton rather than with Bolo, whom she complements, is narrated as a symbolic rejection of the village's complex construction of gender, where masculinity and femininity are represented as integrated, mutually enhancing characteristics rather than as antagonistic and mutually exclusive principles. Narrative comment provided by Eva corroborates this assessment:

> Poor Eulalie. Some say she was a fool to throw 'way her chances with Bolo, who she know, and go with Ivan Morton. But when I look at it, I see that what happen with Eulalie was showing something bigger was happening in the village right under our nose. What was happening was that the warrior was dying in the village as the chief figure. (*WA*, 46)

Eva's sense of the village warrior dying does not automatically assert the notion of the warrior as male. She understands that the village warriorhood, represented as a complex integration in each individual of stereotypical masculine and feminine traits, has been subverted by colonialism's binarist representation of such traits as antagonistic and competing principles. Bolo recognizes that the village's repressed masculinity necessitates an exaggerated display of aggressive behavior. Significantly, for his final act of violence against his own people, Bolo chooses Primus, who more than any other man in the village represents a hyper-feminine passivity in contradistinction to the hyper-masculine assertions of the oppressive colonial power. Bolo intends to use the confrontation with Primus to resurrect the village's displaced masculine traits, but the villagers fail yet again to accept his challenge. The final confrontation between the villagers and Bolo results not only in his death but in the death of Primus's young daughter, Muriel.

The symbolism of this dual sacrifice, male and female, suggests that a sustained binarist representation of stereotypical masculine and feminine traits, where such a configuration establishes these gendered traits as antagonistic polarities rather than as a complex synthesis, eventually leads to a disintegration of individual and community. The dual sacrifice which is really a composite offering to the Spirit of the Shouter Baptist church is finally unworthy because the Shouter Baptist faithful have waited too long to resist the prohibition ordinance. As a result of sustained compromise in the presence of repressive colonial demands, the pastor, Bee, has engendered a disjunction between masculine and feminine traits. Thus, the final thematic emphasis of the novel focuses upon the departure of the Spirit from the Shouter Baptist congregation and reveals its remanifestation in the steel-pan (steel-drum) yard. The shift is from the religious to the secular world, but the Spirit is the same.

In conclusion, *The Wine of Astonishment*, moreso than *Natural Rebels*, manages to provide an imaginative reading of a historical circumstance by reaching behind historical data as well as ideological norms. Lovelace's text, like Morrison's *Beloved*, provides the reader with a glimpse of the ways in which narratives can renew historical fact and rescue human agency from disciplinary and discursive limitations by "playing out the problem as the solution" rather than by seeking new and definitive solutions through the use of dominant discursive structures. Such struggle with discursive and disciplinary structures clearly seeks to reach behind the "dead hand" of narratives of dominance in order to give voice and presence to human intelligence and imagination understood as premium modalities of functional existence.

Notes

1. Rex Nettleford, *Inward Stretch, Outward Reach: A Voice from the Caribbean* (New York: Caribbean Diaspora Press, 1993), viii.

2. Gayatri Spivak, *In Other Worlds: Essays in Cultural Politics* (New York: Routledge, 1988), 77.

3. Gayatri Spivak, Translator's preface, in Jacques Derrida, *Of Grammatology* (Baltimore, Md.: Johns Hopkins University Press, 1974), xiii.

4. Spivak, *In Other Worlds*, 77.

5. See W. E. B. DuBois, *The Souls of Black Folk*, ed. Henry Louis Gates Jr. and Terri Hume Oliver (New York: Norton, 1999), 10–11.

6. Hilary McD. Beckles, *Natural Rebels: A Social History of Enslaved Black Women in Barbados* (New Brunswick, N.J.: Rutgers University Press, 1989), 4–5. Hereafter *NR*, cited in the text.

7. Bridget Brereton, "Searching for the Invisible Woman," *Slavery and Abolition* 13, no. 2 (August 1992): 89. Hereafter "SIW," cited in the text.

8. Elizabeth Fox-Genovese, "Unspeakable Things Unspoken: Ghosts and Memories in the Narratives of African-American Women," *The 1992 Elsa Goveia Memorial Lecture* (Kingston: Department of History, University of the West Indies, 1993), 4–5. Hereafter "UTU," cited in the text.

9. Ashis Nandy, *The Intimate Enemy: Loss and Recovery of Self under Colonialism* (Delhi: Oxford University Press, 1983), 37–38.

10. Earl Lovelace, *The Wine of Astonishment* (London: Heinemann, 1983), 21. Hereafter *WA*, cited in the text.

DATE DUE